Meaning
A play based on the life of Viktor E. Frankl

Rubin Battino, M.S.
Mental Health Counseling
Adjunct Professor,
Department of Human Services (counseling)
Wright State University, Ohio, USA

Crown House Publishing
www.crownhouse.co.uk

Crown House Publishing Limited
Crown Buildings
Bancyfelin
Carmarthen
Wales
SA33 5ND
UK

Crown House Publishing Limited
P.O. Box 2223
Williston
VT 05495-2223
USA

www.crownhouse.co.uk

British Library Cataloguing-in-Publication Data
A catalogue entry for this book is available
from the British Library.

International Standard Book Number
1899836837

Library of Congress Control Number
2002107638

Printed and bound in the UK by
Bell & Bain Limited
Glasgow

Dedication

To Viktor E. Frankl and his wife Elly, for just being who they are
and for what they've given humanity.

Table of Contents

Acknowledgments

Permission to use and adapt Frankl's words for this biographical drama from the following sources is gratefully acknowledged:

Frankl, V.E., *The Doctor and the Soul. From Psychotherapy to Logotherapy* (New York: Vintage Books (Random House), 1955/1986).

Frankl, V.E., *Man's Search for Meaning* (New York: Simon and Schuster, 1959/1984).

Frankl, V.E., *Psychotherapy and Existentialism* (New York: Washington Square Press (Pocket Books), 1967).

Frankl, V.E., *The Will to Meaning. Foundations and Applications of Logotherapy* (New York: A Meridian Book (Plume) 1969/1988).

Frankl, V.E., *The Unheard Cry for Meaning* (New York: A Touchstone Book (Simon and Schuster, 1978).

Frankl, V.E., *Viktor Frankl. Recollections. An Autobiography* (Cambridge, MA: Perseus Publishing, 2000).

We gratefully acknowledge the following sources for the photographs reproduced in this book.

Bartoszewski, W. (1968). *Warsaw Death Ring. 1939–1944.* Drukarnia Zwiazkowa w Krakowie, Poland.

Frankl, V.E. (2000). *Viktor Frankl. Recollections. An Autobiography.* Cambridge, MA: Perseus Publishing.

Zelizer, B. (2000). *Visual Culture and The Holocaust.* New Brunswick, NJ: Rutgers University Press.

Klingberg, H. (2001). *When Life Calls Out to Us. The Love and Lifework of Viktor and Elly Frankl.* New York: Doubleday.

Fischel, J.R. (1998). *The Holocaust.* Westport, CT: Greenwood Press.

Hartmann, E. (1995). *In the Camps.* New York: W.W. Norton & Company.

Poznanski, S. (1963). *Struggle, Death, Memory. 1939–1945.* Warsaw, Poland: P.P. Wydawnictwa Artystyczne I Filmowe (Artistic and Film Publications, State Enterprise).

Viktor Frankl Institute, Langwiesgasse 6, A-1140, Vienna, Austria.

Foreword

Albert Camus wrote in *The First Man*, "There are people who vindicate the world, who help others just by their presence."

For those of us who have encountered these precious souls who seem to "vindicate the world," it may be difficult to describe the qualities that make them different from others, but we know when we have been touched by them. Their mere presence seems to charge the moment, giving sudden depth and clarity to simply being alive. Often, these people have suffered greatly; they are the wounded healers who have taken their own suffering and made it a resource from which to draw the strength and empathy to help others.

Viktor Frankl was a man whose presence vindicated the world. I was privileged to know him and his family. I was among the multitudes who admired him, learned from him, and loved him unabashedly. I am a better man for having known him.

As a psychologist, I try to define the driving passion of such prodigious souls. What is it that allows a human being to bear, and even to transcend, seemingly unbearable burdens—to thrive where another might wither? For Frankl, the answer was in a simple little word that contains the world: *meaning*. He was the high priest of meaning, and it was a sacred word to him, without which there could be no true motivation.

Viktor E. Frankl, M.D., Ph.D., was born in Vienna, Austria, on March 26, 1905, and he died there on September 2, 1997. He was Professor of Neurology and Psychiatry at the University of Vienna. A guest professor at several universities in the United States, he held 29 honorary doctorates from universities throughout the world. During World War II, he spent three years at Auschwitz, Dachau, and other concentration camps. Frankl's 32 books appear in 26 languages. According to a Library of Congress poll, his *Man's Search for Meaning* is one of the ten most influential books among readers in the United States.

Frankl was the founder of Logotherapy, the third Viennese school of psychiatry, Freudian and Adlerian being the other two. Logotherapy maintains that there are three main avenues to creating meaning in life: the first is through deeds and working; the second is through relationships (loving and experiences); and the third is through facing a difficult fate and then building upon that challenge in order to help others.

Meaning: A Play Based on the Life of Viktor Frankl brings Frankl to life in full dimension—his spirit, determination, wisdom, and integrity. Battino has chosen to set the play for the most part during the Holocaust, bringing into sharp focus the extraordinary power of this man to extract from the bleakest of circumstances a reason to live. After all, in contradiction, there is inherent drama. And, while this is a play written in homage to Viktor Frankl, it is, more than that, a play about love and meaning, no matter that reality seems to be calling for something quite different. In these pages, we are reminded of what it is to live profoundly, as we have the opportunity to be in Frankl's presence once again.

Jeffrey K. Zeig, Ph.D.
Director of The Milton H. Erickson Foundation,
President of Zeig, Tucker & Theisen, Inc., Publishers.

Preface

I have visited Vienna many times. On one of those occasions, perhaps fifteen or more years ago, I had occasion to call Dr Frankl to ask if I could see him. He invited me to a lecture he was giving to some visiting Americans. Afterwards, we chatted briefly. He was as I expected: charming, witty, erudite, and full of an irrepressible passion for life. He exuded energy, vitality, and compassion. I had read many of his books, listened repeatedly to audiotapes, and watched him on videotapes. At another time in an audience of more than five thousand therapists in Anaheim when he received a standing ovation *before* he talked.

At some point I conceived of the idea of writing a play about Frankl and his life. (As a hobby, I participate in community theater and have written more than one dozen plays.) On a trip to Vienna about six years ago I called and was graciously invited to visit with him and then to join him and his wife Elly for lunch. After some conversation I broached the idea of writing a play. Frankl rightly surmised that I was requesting his permission for this project, maybe even his blessing! The idea of a "blessing" may appear to be unusual, but there is in Jewish tradition the idea of the *Lamed-Vov*, 36 unknown saintly men who are alive at any given time. It is on their behalf that God allows the world to continue to exist. To my mind, Frankl was one of this group. In response to my query, he responded quite appropriately that I was, of course, free to write whatever I wished—I did not need his approval or permission. We had a lovely lunch at a nearby Italian restaurant. Although Frankl's family have seen this play, that is all.

Before I began to write, I had the challenge of how to organize in dramatic form a presentation of this man's life. Reading his autobiography (1997, and see other references below) and his most famous book, *Man's Search for Meaning* (1984), told me that the most dramatic parts of his life were the war years spent in Nazi concentration camps. The rest of his long and productive life seemed to be an elaboration of the themes discovered in his youth, which were expanded and consolidated during the concentration camp years. The play would have few characters. In explaining the project to my niece Katharine Solomon and my wife, I hit upon the idea of writing the play in a Brechtian style with many scenes illustrated by projected photographs on a bare stage, and with title boards indicating the nature of each scene. So, there are 24 scenes, mostly set in the concentration camps. (For a complete and authorized biography of the Frankls, see Klingberg (2001). Zeig, Tucker & Co., Inc. (3618 North 24th Street, Phoenix, AZ 85016. 877-850-0442, orders@zeigtucker.com), are the official source for all of Frankl's audio and video tapes.)

But, what do you do for dialogue? I chose to use Frankl's writings, mostly from *Man's Search for Meaning*, to be as authentic to his speech as was possible. Frankl needed a foil, and this developed into Frankl's Colleague, a person who has many roles—colleague, interviewer, reporter, biographer, alter ego, conscience. Much of the Colleague's dialogue is also from Frankl's writings. As a playwright, I had to take some liberties to make the dialogue smooth, dramatic, and with appropriate transitions and connections. Yet the words in this play are mostly Frankl's.

Frankl died peacefully on September 2, 1997.

The play was improved by comments made by the members of our monthly play-reading group. Thus, I owe thanks to: Donna and Al Denman, Barbara and Dave Case, Helen and David Westneat, Mary and Len Cargan, Molly and Keith Gunderkline, Martha Kline, and my wife Charlotte.

The support of my editor at Crown House Publishing, Bridget Shine, was unwavering. She finally convinced the editorial board that a biographical play would be appropriate for them to add to their list. The board did not know what to do with a play, but a biography in play form was acceptable!

Thank you, Bridget.

References

Frankl, V.E., *Man's Search for Meaning* (New York: Simon and Schuster, 1959/1984).

Frankl, V.E., *Viktor Frankl. Recollections. An Autobiography* (Cambridge, MA: Perseus Publishing, 2000).

Klingberg, H., *When Life Calls Out to Us. The Love and Lifework of Viktor and Elly Frankl* (New York: Doubleday, 2001).

Rubin Battino
Yellow Springs, Ohio
December 2001

Production Notes

Characters

Professor Viktor E. Frankl (Frankl)
Frankl's Colleague (Colleague)
Capo
Man
Inmate
Foreman
Guard
Woman
Science Teacher
Frau Kotek
Frankl's Father
Old Doctor

Time

Mostly during World War II in the concentration camps.

List of scenes

Act I
Scene 1: About Man's Search for Meaning
Scene 2: A Selection Process: Camp to Camp
Scene 3: Premium Coupons
Scene 4: The First Phase is Shock
Scene 5: The Bath—Textbooks Tell Lies!
Scene 6: Suicide
Scene 7: Apathy—The Second Stage
Scene 8: Dreams and Food
Scene 9: Politics and Religion
Scene 10: My Wife's Image
Scene 11: The Inner Life of the Prisoner
Scene 12: Psychological Factors in the Camps
Scene 13: Being a Typhus Doctor and Acting Like a Sheep
Scene 14: The Science Teacher

Intermission

Act II

Set and production

The play is performed on a bare stage. There are high stools for Frankl and Colleague. It is anticipated that the play will be done as a staged reading rather than have the cast memorize lines. The subsidiary characters sit on chairs arranged at stage right and stage left, and do several roles. Upstage center is a large screen on which appropriate slides are projected. The directions for each scene indicate the slides to be used. Some scenes use several slides. In the book version, photos are included in each scene. There is a smaller screen set at an angle, easily seen by the audience, and above the actors on stage right. On to this screen is projected the title of each scene and other relevant information like dates and settings. This information is indicated under "Title Board" at the beginning of each scene. The Title Board also indicates the characters in each scene. There are specific stage directions under "Stage Directions" at the beginning of each scene. There are 24 scenes in the play. If an intermission is needed, it can be after Scene 14.

The entire production is somewhat Brechtian in style. The setting is stark. Scene 22 is presented in two parts: since Frankl's philosophy is densely written and requires careful reading, only the nonitalicized parts of Scene 22 are meant to be performed—the rest is for more studious reading. Almost all of Frankl's dialogue is taken verbatim from his writings, so that it is really Frankl who is speaking throughout. The author has taken a few liberties for dramatic effect in introducing Frankl's Colleague and the sequencing of the scenes. Frankl's Colleague takes on many roles during the course of the play. He is a colleague, an interviewer and reporter, a biographer, and an alter ego—sometimes even Frankl's conscience. Some of Colleague's lines are actually taken from Frankl's writings. In a staged production, Frankl's voice (from one of his many lectures) is heard at the end of the play.

Frankl, of course, led a long and productive life following his liberation from the concentration camps. The author makes no excuse for focusing the play on those events and times that were the crucible for Frankl's enormous contributions to mankind. There are even some who say that Frankl was one of the Lamed-Vov of Jewish legend. This legend states that at any given time there are 36 hidden saints known as the Just Men. The mission of these Just Men was to roam the earth caring about human suffering, knowing they could do nothing to relieve it. Jewish tradition holds that, as long as this caring goes on, God would allow the world of ordinary people to continue to exist. Frankl was more than a Lamed-Vov since his life and contributions did much to alleviate suffering.

Act I

Scene 1

About Man's Search
for Meaning

Title Board:	**ABOUT MAN'S SEARCH FOR MEANING**
	In a lecture hall
	Frankl; Frankl's Colleague
Visual:	Frankl lecturing.
Stage Directions:	There is a lectern for a lecture. Frankl is behind the lectern and Colleague is stage right commenting.

FRANKL: My book *Man's Search for Meaning* does not claim to be an account of facts and events but of personal experiences, experiences which millions of prisoners here suffered time and again. It is the inside story of a concentration camp, told by one of its survivors. This tale is not concerned with the great horrors, which have already been described often enough (though less often believed), but with the multitude of small torments. In other words, it will try to answer this question: How was everyday life in a concentration camp reflected in the mind of the average prisoner?

FRANKL'S COLLEAGUE (COLLEAGUE): And you presume to speak for them all, to describe their experiences? You survived, yes. Speak about your thoughts, your survival. Do you think another description will answer that question?

FRANKL: Yes. We were separate, we were individual, we made choices; yet, we were so controlled and confined that at times we were just one mind, one body.

COLLEAGUE: So tell your tale. On your head be it.

FRANKL: Most of the events described in the book did not take place in the large and famous camps, but in the small ones where most of the real extermination took place. This story is not about the suffering and death of great heroes and martyrs, nor is it about the prominent Capos—prisoners who acted as trustees, having special privileges—or well-known prisoners. It is not so much concerned with the suffering of the mighty, but with the sacrifices, the crucifixion and the deaths of the great army of unknown and unrecorded victims.

COLLEAGUE: You're reading minds again.

FRANKL: Not so, we were one. Yes, it was these common prisoners, who bore no distinguishing marks on their sleeves, whom the Capos really despised. You see, while these ordinary prisoners had little or nothing to eat, the Capos never went hungry. In fact, many of the Capos lived better in the camp than they had in their lives.

COLLEAGUE: Another paradox.

FRANKL: Often these men were harder on the prisoners than were the guards, and beat them more cruelly than the SS men did.

COLLEAGUE: And will you tell their story, too?

FRANKL: Perhaps that will come out. These Capos, of course, were chosen only from those prisoners whose characters promised to make them suitable for such procedures. If they did not comply with what was expected of them, they were immediately demoted.

COLLEAGUE: They, too, had choices; or did fear rob them of that?

FRANKL: Fear? Fear? Almost a meaningless word in the camps.

COLLEAGUE: You were afraid.

FRANKL: Of course. You would need to be crazy not to. But, these men soon became much like the SS men and the camp wardens. They can all be judged on a similar psychological basis.

COLLEAGUE: Are you judging? You who understood it all?

FRANKL: You can understand *and* judge. That is what makes us human. To understand does not remove the obligation to judge. Or to forgive.

Wednesday Lecture, 1966.
Source: Viktor Frankl Institute, Vienna, Austria.

COLLEAGUE: Fancy words. I need to hear more.

FRANKL: Nietzsche said, "He who has a *why* to live for can bear with almost any *how*."

COLLEAGUE: Fancy thought, nicely phrased. Out of what concentration camp did Nietzsche come?

FRANKL: You do not have to suffer to learn. But, if you don't learn from suffering over which you have no control, then your life becomes truly meaningless.

COLLEAGUE: You don't recommend suffering for learning?

FRANKL: Only if it is beyond your control ...

End of Scene 1

Frankl, 1994.

Scene 2

A Selection Process: Camp to Camp

Title Board:	**A SELECTION PROCESS**
	Moving from one camp to another
	Capo; Frankl; Man; Colleague
Visual:	A camp scene outside the huts.
Stage Directions:	Standing and talking before the screen. Frankl and Colleague are joined by Man. The Capo leaves after his opening lines.

Camp.
Source: Hartmann, E. (1995). In the Camps.

CAPO: Tomorrow morning we will be moving fifty of you to another camp. This is a rest camp where you don't work so hard. There are even doctors and some nurses. I've been told they even have some medicine. We'll make the selection tonight. Think about it—a rest camp. It's hard to believe they're so generous. But that's what I've been told. Think about it. I'll consider requests. [*Leaves.*]

FRANKL: They've said that before.

MAN: This Capo is almost honest. Remember when he turned a blind eye? I'm thinking of volunteering.

FRANKL: They'll only take those too weak to work. I'm staying here. You stay, too.

MAN: Who can we get in our place? They just want numbers. Maybe, the bosses want fresh blood to do their work. Too many weak ones here.

FRANKL: We can tell them of our special skills. I'm a doctor.

MAN: So, who needs you here? You have no office, no instruments, no medicines. You'll survive as long as you can move dirt with a shovel, pick a hole. Doctors!

FRANKL: All they think about are our numbers. Can't wash them off. We're only numbers to them. No names. Any guard can make a charge by reading a number.

MAN: There are those six in the corner—they're good for nothing now. We'll give their names.

FRANKL: Is it better we should do the choosing?

COLLEAGUE: Better? Better? At least when they choose there's some kind of crazy logic—take the weakest and the sickest. Once you start choosing, Viktor, you are no different than the Capos. No different, you hear?

FRANKL: I must stay alive for my family, to help my friends here.

COLLEAGUE: Keep talking.

FRANKL: There is my work, the book, my whole life. My wife.

COLLEAGUE: Keep talking. You'll convince yourself. You've written something for the book in your head.

FRANKL: Yes. Yes. Listen. With no hesitation a prisoner would arrange for another prisoner, another "number," to take his place in the transport. The process of selecting the Capos was a negative one; only the most brutal of the prisoners were chosen for this job, although there were some happy exceptions—very few, very few. Apart from the selection of the Capos by the SS, there was a sort of self-selecting process going on the whole time among the prisoners. On the average, only those prisoners could keep alive who, after years of trekking from camp to camp, had lost all scruples in their fight for existence.

MAN: Who shall we pick?

COLLEAGUE: Think, Viktor, think.

FRANKL: They were prepared to use every means, honest, and otherwise, even brutal force, theft, and betrayal of their friends, in order to save themselves.

COLLEAGUE: Think.

FRANKL: We who have come back, by the aid of many lucky chances or miracles—whatever one may choose to call them—we know: the best of us did not return.

MAN: We have to choose.

FRANKL: I choose not to choose. I've been protected before, chance or miracle or …

COLLEAGUE: You've chosen!

Viktor Frankl, 1940.

End of Scene 2

Scene 3

Premium Coupons

Title Board:	**EARNING PREMIUM COUPONS**
	Just before Christmas 1944
	Colleague; Frankl
Visual:	Group working for a construction firm, digging.
Stage Directions:	Play "Die Moorsoldaten" (the peat bog soldiers) softly in the background.

Trench digging. Source: Poznanski, S. (1963). Struggle, Death, Memory. 1939–1945.

COLLEAGUE: You were a psychiatrist. What did you do in the camps?

FRANKL: I'm going to tell you, not without pride, that I was not employed as a psychiatrist in the camp. Or even as a doctor, except for the last few weeks. Some of my colleagues were lucky enough to be employed in poorly heated first-aid posts, applying bandages made of scraps of waste paper. But I was Number 119,104, and most of the time I was digging and laying tracks for railway lines.

11

COLLEAGUE: You survived as a number, digging real dirt rather than that buried in the souls of your captors.

FRANKL: Have it your way. At one time, my job was to dig a tunnel, without help, for a water main under the road. This feat did not go unrewarded.

COLLEAGUE: How so?

FRANKL: Just before Christmas 1944, I was presented with a gift of so-called "premium coupons." These were issued by the construction firm to which we were practically sold as slaves. The firm paid the camp authorities a fixed price per day, per prisoner.

COLLEAGUE: Generous of them.

FRANKL: The coupons cost the firm fifty pfennigs each and could be exchanged for six cigarettes, often weeks later. I became the proud owner of a token worth twelve cigarettes. Imagine that!

COLLEAGUE: You can't live on cigarettes.

FRANKL: Ah, but the cigarettes could be exchanged for twelve soups and—

COLLEAGUE: —and that made the difference between starving and—

FRANKL: No. Not starving. Just a brief respite from starving. Just a brief respite.

COLLEAGUE: Tell me more about these cigarettes.

FRANKL: Yes. In fact the privilege of actually smoking cigarettes was reserved for the Capo, who had his assured quota of weekly coupons. Sometimes it was for a prisoner who worked as a foreman in a warehouse or a workshop. He received a few cigarettes in exchange for doing dangerous jobs.

COLLEAGUE: How nice.

FRANKL: There was an exception. This was for those who had lost the will to live and wanted to "enjoy" their last days. When we saw a comrade smoking his own cigarettes, we knew he had given up faith in his strength to carry on. Once that faith was lost, the will to live seldom returned.

COLLEAGUE: The condemned man smoking his last cigarette?

FRANKL: We were all condemned. They made this their last choice.

Frankl in New York, 1968.

End of Scene 3

Scene 4

The First Phase is Shock

Title Board:	**THE FIRST PHASE IS SHOCK**
	Arriving at Auschwitz
	Frankl; Colleague; Inmate
Visual:	Cattle cars delivering prisoners. "Selection" process at a camp.
Stage Directions:	Use several slides of prisoners arriving at a camp.

The infamous Dr Mengele at the station at Auschwitz during the "selection."
Source: Frankl, V.E. (1997). Viktor Frankl Recollections. An Autobiography.

FRANKL: The symptom that characterizes the first phase is shock.

COLLEAGUE: You are giving your formal lecture now or reliving?

FRANKL: There is no way to distinguish between the two—when I describe, no matter how scientifically, I am there.

15

Disembarkation at Auschwitz, Birkenau.
Source: Fischel, J.R. (1998). The Holocaust.

COLLEAGUE: Continue.

FRANKL: Fifteen hundred persons had been traveling by train for several days and several nights. There were eighty people in each coach. All had to lie on top of their luggage. The carriages were so full that only the tops of the windows were free to let in the gray light of dawn. The engine's whistle had an uncanny sound, like a cry for help. We didn't know where we were. Then the train shunted. Suddenly, a cry broke out, "There is a sign. Auschwitz!" Everyone's heart missed a beat. Auschwitz—the very name stood for all that was horrible: gas chambers, crematoriums, massacres.

COLLEAGUE: How did they know?

FRANKL: Rumors in the night. That name had a horror.

COLLEAGUE: Go on.

FRANKL: The train moved almost hesitantly, as if it wanted to spare its passengers the realization of Auschwitz. With the

Summer, 1942: Jews being loaded on to a death train in Stawki Street (so called Umschlagplatz).
Source: Bartoszewski, W. (1968). Warsaw Death Ring. 1939–1944.

dawn, the outlines of an immense camp became visible: barbed-wire fences, watchtowers, searchlights. And long columns of ragged human figures, themselves gray in the grayness of the dawn. Walking the desolate roads to where we knew not. There were isolated shouts and whistles of command—we did not know their meaning.

COLLEAGUE: Not knowing is more terrifying than knowing.

FRANKL: Eventually, we moved into the station. Shouted commands. The carriage doors were flung open and a small detachment of prisoners stormed inside. They wore striped uniforms, their heads were shaved, but, surprisingly, they looked well fed. They spoke every European tongue—and all with a certain sense of humor—which sounded grotesque at the time. Like a drowning man my inborn optimism clung to this thought: these prisoners live quite well and even laugh. Who knows? I might share their good fortune.

COLLEAGUE: A delusion. A dangerous delusion.

Cattle cars.
Source: Poznanski, S. (1963). Struggle, Death, Memory.
1939–1945.

FRANKL: Yes. You know, in psychiatry there is a certain condition known as "delusion of reprieve." The condemned man, immediately before his execution, gets the illusion that he might be reprieved at the very last minute. We believed that, too. Those special prisoners fooled us. They were a chosen elite who were this receiving squad. They took charge of us and our belongings; smuggled jewelry filling dead storehouses.

COLLEAGUE: The spoils of war.

FRANKL: Not spoils. Outright robbery, debasement, thievery.

COLLEAGUE: All armies do this.

FRANKL: Not to civilians. Not in modern times.

COLLEAGUE: Be honest. In all times armies did this. Were the Nazis so different?

FRANKL: Yes. They were organized, they were "scientific."

COLLEAGUE: So were the Romans.

FRANKL: I'll not argue with you. Let me continue. We were fifteen hundred people crammed in a space for two hundred. One five-ounce piece of bread in four days. We still lived under the illusion of being reprieved.

COLLEAGUE: Then there was the selection ...

FRANKL: We were told to leave our luggage in the train and to fall into two lines—women on one side, and men on the other. This was to file past a senior SS officer. I had the courage to hide my haversack under my coat. If found, at the minimum I would be knocked down. So, instinctively, I straightened to conceal my heavy load. Then I was face to face with him. He was in a spotless uniform. Spotless. With careless ease, his right arm supported in his left hand, he lifted his right forefinger, leisurely pointing to the right or left.

Cattle cars.
Source: Poznanski, S.
(1963). Struggle, Death, Memory. 1939–1945.

COLLEAGUE: Right or left?

FRANKL: We had no idea what that small gesture foreboded. But, there were more to the left than the right. I just waited for things to take their course.

COLLEAGUE: Fatalism is also an action.

FRANKL: This was the first of many such times—choices beyond my control. I made an effort to walk upright. He looked me over, and then put both hands on my shoulders. I tried very hard to look smart. He turned my shoulders very slowly until I faced right, and I moved over to that side.

[*Have an actor silently do the choosing and do this.*]

19

COLLEAGUE: It was obviously to life. Why did he make that extra choice? Was God's hands guiding his hands? Left or right?

FRANKL: Ninety percent went left—it meant death. A sentence that was carried out within the next few hours. Straight to the crematorium. To the bath.

COLLEAGUE: They were fooled.

FRANKL: Yes. The word "bath" was written on its doors in several languages. In the evening, I asked about a friend.

INMATE: Was he sent to the left side?

FRANKL: Yes.

INMATE: Then you can see him there.

FRANKL: Where?

INMATE: That column of flames from the chimney. That's where your friend is, floating up to Heaven.

FRANKL: I don't understand.

COLLEAGUE: That such evil is possible …

INMATE: Dust to dust. Ashes to ashes. Smoke.

End of Scene 4

Scene 5

The Bath—Textbooks Tell Lies!

Title Board:	**THE CLEANSING STATION AT THE CAMP**
	This was a real bath
	Frankl; Colleague; Inmate; Guard
Visual:	Blurred series of slides showing people stripping and then dressing in odd-sized clothing.
Stage Directions:	Add sound effects of background of showers, dropping shoes, guards giving orders.

FRANKL: They took us to the cleansing station. This was a real bath. The SS men almost seemed charming—another illusion of reprieve. We handed over our watches and other jewelry in hopes of buying a favor.

COLLEAGUE: Illusions. All illusions.

FRANKL: We had to throw all of our possessions in blankets. No one could grasp the idea that nothing was left to us.

INMATE: What do you want?

FRANKL: Look. This is the manuscript of a scientific book in my pocket.

INMATE: So?

FRANKL: I know what you're thinking—I should be grateful to escape with my life.

21

INMATE: A piece of paper.

FRANKL: I cannot help myself. I must keep this manuscript at all costs. It contains my life's work.

INMATE: Shit! That's all that's good for. Shit!

COLLEAGUE: And you lost it all.

GUARD: I will give you two minutes, and I will time you by my watch. In these two minutes you will get fully undressed and drop everything on the floor where you are standing. You will take nothing with you except your shoes, your belt or suspenders, and possibly a truss. I am starting to count—now!

[*Behind the scrim begins the shadow play of tearing off clothes. There is whipping. Heads and bodies are shaved. Then the showers. Some play of covering nakedness. Frankl retains his glasses and his belt, sorting through piles of clothes for some that fit.*]

COLLEAGUE: You found some clothes.

FRANKL: Finding shoes was the hardest.

COLLEAGUE: You were still thinking.

FRANKL: There was a strange kind of humor in the showers and with the clothes. Yet my strongest sensation was curiosity.

Jerzy Potrzebowski: "Selection of the sick for the gas chamber" (Drawing). Source: *Poznanski, S. (1963).* Struggle, Death, Memory. 1939–1945.

Once, when my life was endangered by a climbing accident, I felt only curiosity at the critical moment—curiosity as to whether I should come out of it alive.

COLLEAGUE: This was very different.

FRANKL: Not really. Cold curiosity predominated in Auschwitz. Somehow, detaching the mind from its surroundings was a kind of objectivity. This curiosity evolved into surprise.

COLLEAGUE: Strange.

FRANKL: Strange, but true. In the chill of late autumn, stark naked, wet, and cold. We were surprised that we did not catch cold. Textbooks tell lies.

COLLEAGUE: Tell me more.

FRANKL: Somewhere it is said that man cannot exist without sleep for a certain number of hours. Quite wrong! I had been convinced I could only sleep in a certain way, with certain things.

COLLEAGUE: That's true!

FRANKL: Hah! In Auschwitz we slept in beds constructed in tiers. On each tier which was about six and one-half to eight feet, nine men slept, and directly on the boards. Directly. Only arms which were near to dislocation for pillows. Of course, we could only lie on our sides, crowded and huddled together. This was actually an advantage.

COLLEAGUE: Only you could …

FRANKL: We were all blessed the same way—our meager warmth helped in the cold. Only two blankets for nine men. Yet, sleep always came,

Inside a hut.
Source: Hartmann, E.
(1995). In the Camps.

23

A gas chamber.
Source: Hartmann, E. (1995). In the Camps.

with a peaceful oblivion and a relief from pain for a few
hours.

COLLEAGUE: Any more medical lies?

FRANKL: There was no way to clean our teeth. Despite that and a
severe vitamin deficiency, we had healthier gums than before.
Imagine! We wore the same clothes for months. Also, we
could rarely wash. Somehow, the sores and cuts on our hands
did not suppurate. Frostbite was something else.

COLLEAGUE: You survived.

FRANKL: Don't ask me how. Dostoyevsky defined man as a being
who could get used to anything. We would reply, "Yes, a man
can get used to anything, but do not ask us how." Do not ask
me how.

End of Scene 5

Scene 6

Suicide

Title Board:	**CONTEMPLATING SUICIDE**
	Running into the wire
	Colleague; Frankl; Man
Visual:	Wire fences around camp. Body on fence. Walking tall. Prisoner with crudely shaved face.
Stage Directions:	Series of slides matching the dialogue. End with slides of a prisoner standing tall and proud.

COLLEAGUE: In a place like that I might have killed myself.

FRANKL: Some did. The thought of suicide was entertained by nearly everyone, if only for a brief time. This was born of the hopelessness, the constant danger of capricious death, seeing so many others die daily. We lived, if that is the right word, with death.

COLLEAGUE: Yet, you didn't …

FRANKL: … commit suicide? No. From personal convictions on that first night I made myself a firm promise that I would not "run into the wire."

COLLEAGUE: Explain, please.

FRANKL: Explain, explain. You want words. We lived it. The most popular method of suicide was running into the electrically charged fence. Fast and simple.

COLLEAGUE: Go on.

Fences.
Source: Hartmann, E. (1995). In the Camps.

FRANKL: In another way, there was little point in committing suicide. We knew that our life expectancy was very short. There
were all the "selections." Accidents and diseases, too. After
the first shock, we did not fear death. Even the gas chambers
lost their horrors for us after the first ten days. After all, they
spared us the act of committing suicide.

COLLEAGUE: Your attitude was different.

FRANKL: Perhaps. Friends later told me that I was one whom the
shock of admission did not greatly depress. Let me tell you a
story.

COLLEAGUE: Yes.

FRANKL: A friend smuggled himself into our block to enlighten us. He was so thin, we almost didn't recognize him. He had a good humor and a devil-may-care attitude while he gave us some tips.

MAN: Don't be afraid. Don't fear the selections! They have a soft spot for doctors.

COLLEAGUE: Did they?

FRANKL: Not true. Not true. I can still hear him …

MAN: Shave daily if you can, even if you have to use a piece of glass. Even if you have to use your last piece of bread for it. You will look younger and the scraping will make your cheeks look ruddier. If you want to stay alive, there is only one way: look fit for work. If you even limp, because, let us say, you have a small blister on your heel, and an SS man spots this, he will wave you aside and the next day you will be gassed.

FRANKL: Thank you.

MAN: Do you know what we mean by a "Moslem"? A man who looks miserable, down and out, sick and emaciated, and who cannot manage hard physical labor any longer … That is a "Moslem." Sooner or later, usually sooner, every "Moslem" goes to the gas chambers. Remember: shave, stand and walk smartly, then you need not be afraid of gas. All of you standing here, even if you have only been here twenty-four hours, you need not fear gas, except perhaps for you.

FRANKL: Me?

MAN: I hope you don't mind my telling you frankly.

FRANKL: No.

MAN: You see, of all of you he is the only one who must fear the next selection. So, don't worry!

FRANKL: [*Smiling.*] Thank you, you really are a good man.

End of Scene 6

Scene 7

Apathy—The Second Stage

Title Board:	APATHY—THE SECOND STAGE
	Survival
	Colleague; Frankl; Foreman
Visual:	Digging latrines. Beating prisoners. In a hut. Talking to a Capo.
Stage Directions:	Match visuals to dialogue. End up with talking to a Capo.

COLLEAGUE: You talk about stages, the changes all of the inmates went through. Were these fast?

FRANKL: Well, the second stage developed quite rapidly. In just a few days we all developed a relative apathy, a kind of emotional death.

COLLEAGUE: Just too numb to react.

FRANKL: It was the hopelessness, the degradation, the constant exposure to death and deprivation and torture. It never stopped and there was no escape.

COLLEAGUE: Except running into the wire.

FRANKL: Let me give you an example. A new arrival was usually assigned to a work group to clean the latrines and remove the sewage. It frequently happened that some of the excrement splashed into his face during its transport. Any sign of disgust, an attempt to wipe it off was punished by a blow from a Capo.

COLLEAGUE: You were shit.

29

FRANKL: No escape. No escape from those things.

COLLEAGUE: So, you became hardened.

FRANKL: Of course. That was survival. At first we couldn't look at prisoners being punished; maybe just walking up and down for hours in the mire. In no more than a few weeks, you did not avert your eyes from these scenes. Feelings were blunted, and you watched unmoved.

COLLEAGUE: A kind of protective dissociation.

FRANKL: We just did not see it any more. Survival. When a man died, one by one the prisoners approached the still warm body. One took what food there was. Another traded shoes or a coat. And another was glad to secure some string—just imagine—genuine string! I watched with unconcern, like everyone else. I may have spoken to that man an hour ago—now I just continued sipping my soup. I am even surprised now that I remember that.

COLLEAGUE: You also had to survive beatings.

FRANKL: Of course. Beatings occurred on the slightest provocation, sometimes for no reason at all. Strangely, a blow for no reason can hurt more than one that is earned. Once I was mending a railroad track in a snowstorm. I worked hard since that was a way to keep warm. For only one moment I paused to get my breath and lean on my shovel. The guard turned round then, saw me, and thought I was loafing. The pain he caused me was not from any insults or any blows.

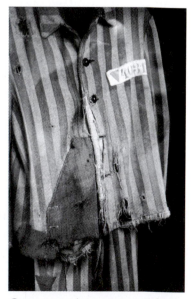

Concentration camp uniform. Source: Hartmann, E. (1995). In the Camps.

Inside a concentration camp hut. Source: Poznanski, S. (1963). Struggle, Death, Memory. 1939–1945.

He did not think it worthwhile to say anything, not even a swear word, to that ragged and emaciated figure standing before him. He threw a stone at me, like you would to get the attention of a dumb beast.

COLLEAGUE: Unbearable. Unbearable.

FRANKL: Another time we were in a forest, digging, with the temperature at two Fahrenheit. There was a foreman with chubby rosy cheeks.

FOREMAN: You, pig. I have been watching you the whole time! I'll teach you to work, yet! Wait till you dig dirt with your teeth— you'll die like an animal! In two days, I'll finish you off! You haven't done a stroke of work in your life. What were you, swine? A businessman?

FRANKL: I was a doctor, a specialist.

FOREMAN: What? A doctor? I bet you got a lot of money out of people.

FRANKL: No. As it happens, I did most of my work for no money at all, in clinics for the poor.

[*Foreman screams and shouts and beats Frankl.*]

COLLEAGUE: A crazy man.

Clandestine image of Sonderkommando forced to burn bodies in Birkenau. Source: Zelizer, B. (2000). Visual Culture and The Holocaust.

FRANKL: No, that is not the point. It wasn't about the cruelty and pain. It was the insult. I had to listen to a man judge my life who had so little idea of it. No understanding at all.

COLLEAGUE: Yet again you survived.

FRANKL: The Capo in that group saved me. This happened a number of times—I don't know why.

COLLEAGUE: "Whys" can be dangerous.

FRANKL: One Capo had taken a liking to me because I listened to his love stories and matrimonial troubles. He poured them out during the long marches to our work site.

COLLEAGUE: Just listening can help.

FRANKL: Yes. But I also made an impression on him with my diagnosis of his character and with my psychotherapeutic advice. I was very happy to be the personally appointed physician to His Honor the Capo!

End of Scene 7

Scene 8

Dreams and Food

Title Board:	**DREAMS AND FOOD**
	Colleague; Frankl; Man
Visual:	Food lines in camp. Eating in a hut. Restaurant in color. Meal at home in color. Bakery window. Supermarket.
Stage Directions:	Alternate camp photos in black and white of people eating with color photos of bakery, restaurant, supermarket, festive meal at home. Fade through with a fuzzy focus from one to the other.

COLLEAGUE: In those hard times did you still dream?

FRANKL: Yes, yes. Of course. Our wishes and desires became obvious in our dreams.

COLLEAGUE: What did the prisoners dream about most frequently?

FRANKL: Oh, we dreamed about bread, cake, cigarettes—and nice warm baths. We sought wish-fulfillment in dreams. Did they do any good? After all, the dreamer had to wake from them to the reality of camp life, to those terrible constraints.

COLLEAGUE: Yet you kept dreaming.

FRANKL: Yes. I shall never forget how I was roused one night by the groans of a fellow prisoner. He was throwing himself about in his sleep, obviously having a terrible nightmare.

COLLEAGUE: What did you do?

33

FRANKL: I wanted to wake the poor man since I had always been especially sorry for people who suffered from fearful dreams or deliria.

COLLEAGUE: And?

FRANKL: And I suddenly drew back the hand which was ready to shake him. I was frightened at the thing I was about to do.

COLLEAGUE: Why?

FRANKL: You see, at that moment I became intensely conscious of the fact that no dream, no matter how horrible, could be as bad as the reality of the camp which surrounded us. No dream.

COLLEAGUE: I see. But your dreams about food?

FRANKL: Well, the desire for food was the major primitive instinct around which mental life centered. If they were not closely watched, they would immediately start discussing food.

A concentration camp day-room table.
Source: Hartmann, E. (1995). In the Camps.

MAN: What are you favorite dishes?

FRANKL: You tell me now.

MAN: I have some wonderful recipes for you. Look, let's plan our menu for tomorrow. We'll start with breakfast.

FRANKL: Good, good.

MAN: Oh, oh, what a reunion we'll have when this is all over. Tables just loaded with food. All kinds of breads, piled high in baskets. Fresh baked, crisp, full of bread smells.

FRANKL: Yes.

MAN: And other tables loaded with cheeses, soft and hard and in between. Meats, fruits, vegetables. Strawberries, endless bowls, bright red, just ripe, and bowls of cream.

FRANKL: The guard is coming.

MAN: Not now. Please God, not now.

COLLEAGUE: Those could be dangerous illusions.

FRANKL: I always regarded such talk about food as dangerous. Those images did not connect with our extremely small rations. Our bodies adapted to nonexistent calories.

COLLEAGUE: Yet you survived.

FRANKL: Some of us. Some of us. The daily ration consisted of very watery soup given out once daily, and the usual small bread ration.

COLLEAGUE: That's all?

FRANKL: No. There was usually a so-called "extra allowance" of three-fourths of an ounce of margarine, or a slice of poor-quality sausage, or a little piece of cheese, a bit of synthetic honey, or a spoonful of watery jam. These varied daily. An absolutely inadequate number of calories.

COLLEAGUE: It was something.

FRANKL: No. You must consider our heavy manual work, our constant exposure to cold, and our inadequate clothing. Most of us had edema and our feet barely fit in our unlaced shoes.

COLLEAGUE: So shoes were a major problem.

FRANKL: One morning I heard someone, whom I knew to be brave and dignified, cry like a child because he finally had to go to the snowy marching grounds in his bare feet, as his shoes were too shrunken for him to wear.

COLLEAGUE: And you?

FRANKL: What? Oh, yes. A strange thing. In these ghastly minutes, I found a little bit of comfort: a small piece of bread which I drew out of my pocket and munched with absorbed delight.

COLLEAGUE: A small piece of bread.

FRANKL: Our longing wasn't for the sake of good food itself, but for the sake of knowing that the subhuman existence, which had made us unable to think of anything other than food, would at last cease.

COLLEAGUE: Having plentiful food was a symbol. You talked about two schools of thought.

FRANKL: Yes. One was in favor of eating up the ration immediately. I finally joined the ranks of the second group, dividing up the ration, even with the danger of possible theft or loss.

COLLEAGUE: In your dreams, was there no sexual urge?

FRANKL: Sexual urge? In that environment! Undernourishment did away with it. Also, in those all-male camps there was little sexual perversion.

COLLEAGUE: Strange and not strange. Yet, having to concentrate on saving your skin must have made everything else …

FRANKL: … secondary. Survival, and important dreams. Things and people to live for. To live for …

Notes from Dachau.
Source: Viktor Frankl Institute, Vienna, Austria.

End of Scene 8

Scene 9

Politics and Religion

Title Board: **POLITICS AND RELIGION**

                              Colleague; Frankl

Visual: Group debating. Group praying. But in camp clothes.

Stage Directions: Slowly dissolve from debating photo to praying one.

Buchenwald, April, 1945. Photo by Margaret Bourke-White.
Source: Zelizer, B. (2000). Visual Culture and The Holocaust.

COLLEAGUE: You must have talked about something.

FRANKL: Would you believe politics and religion?

COLLEAGUE: In a death camp?

FRANKL: The politics were based chiefly on rumors. Particularly about the military situation. It was the incorrigible optimists who were the most irritating companions.

COLLEAGUE: That was the politics?

FRANKL: Rumors. There were no papers.

COLLEAGUE: And religion?

FRANKL: Our religious interactions were the most sincere imaginable. There were improvised prayers and services in the most unlikely places: a corner of a hut, a locked cattle truck bringing us back from a distant work site, within our minds snatches of forgotten prayers.

COLLEAGUE: Those with the strongest religious beliefs survived?

FRANKL: Not always, but it always helped. It always helped.

Miecszylaw Koscielniak: "Prayers beside a dead man" (Print). Source: Poznanski, S (1963). Struggle, Death, Memory. 1939–1945.

End of Scene 9

Scene 10

My Wife's Image

Title Board:	**MY WIFE'S IMAGE**
	Guard; Colleague; Man; Frankl
Visual:	Tilly Frankl. Wedding photo. Sign at entrance of Auschwitz, *"Arbeit Macht Frei."* Photo of men digging.
Stage Directions:	Go through slides, matching to dialogue, and end up with photo of Tilly Frankl.

GUARD: Keep moving you slackers. Move.

COLLEAGUE: They are moving. Can't you see? In the dark, over large stones, through icy puddles, with sore feet, some with no shoes.

GUARD: Keep moving. I have shoes, warm clothes. No matter. But these dead people, hah! Maybe get them to dig a little. Move there, you. Can't you walk on your own? I'll teach you …

COLLEAGUE: What do you know of them, their inner lives, their loves, their passions?

GUARD: Numbers, that's all they are. Numbers. Move on there.

MAN: [*Whispering.*] If our wives could see us now! I do hope they are better off in their camps and don't know what is happening to us.

COLLEAGUE: What are you thinking, Frankl?

FRANKL: Of my wife. I knew that each of us was thinking of his wife. Occasionally, I looked at the sky, where the stars were

41

Tilly Frankl.
Source: Frankl, V.E. (1997). Viktor Frankl Recollections. An Autobiography.

fading and the pink light of the morning was beginning to spread behind a dark bank of clouds.

COLLEAGUE: And?

FRANKL: And my mind clung to my wife's image, imagining it with an uncanny acuteness. I heard her answering me, saw her smile, her frank and encouraging look. Real or not, her look was then more luminous than the sun which was beginning to rise.

GUARD: Move. Move. What do you see up there?

FRANKL: A thought transfixed me. The first time in my life I saw the truth as it is set into song by so many poets, and philosophers—the truth that love is the ultimate and the highest goal to which man can aspire.

GUARD: A good kick is what you need. Get up. Move.

FRANKL: Then I grasped the meaning of the greatest secret that human poetry and human thought and belief have to impart: *The salvation of man is through love and in love.*

GUARD: Thinking again, are you? Take that and that! March.

FRANKL: Yes, thank you for the blows. Thank you.

COLLEAGUE: You thanked him?

FRANKL: Inside. You see, I now understood how a man who has nothing left in this world may still know bliss—be it only for a brief moment—in the contemplation of his beloved. In a position of utter desolation, when man cannot express himself in positive action, when his only achievement may consist in enduring his suffering in the right way—an honorable way—in such a position man can, through loving contemplation of the image he carries of his beloved, achieve fulfillment.

COLLEAGUE: You finally learned.

FRANKL: Yes. For the first time in my life I was able to understand the meaning of the words, "The angels are lost in perpetual contemplation of an infinite glory."

GUARD: Fall down, will you? Take that. And you clods falling on him. Get up. Get up. March. *Arbeit Macht frei*. You hear, *Arbeit Macht frei*. March.

COLLEAGUE: He interrupted you.

FRANKL: For a moment, but soon my soul found its way back and I resumed talk with my loved one. I asked her questions, and she answered. She questioned me in return and I answered.

GUARD: Stop! Get your tools. No fighting. Dig. Dig.

FRANKL: We assaulted the frozen ground. Sparks flew from our pickaxes. My comrades were silent, brains numb.

COLLEAGUE: But you couldn't stop your thoughts.

FRANKL: My mind still clung to the image of my wife. A thought crossed my mind: I didn't even know if she were alive. I knew only one thing: Love goes very far

Arbeit Macht Frei.
Source: Hartmann, E. (1995).
In the Camps.

43

beyond the physical person of the beloved. It finds its deepest meaning in his spiritual being, his inner self. Whether or not he is actually present, whether or not he is still alive at all, ceases somehow to be of importance.

GUARD: Dig. You must dig. *Arbeit Macht frei.*

COLLEAGUE: You did not know.

FRANKL: I did not know whether my wife was alive or not, and I had no means of finding out, but at that moment it ceased to matter.

COLLEAGUE: Strange.

FRANKL: Strange, perhaps. But, there was no need for me to know; nothing could touch the strength of my love, my thoughts, and the image of my beloved. Had I known then that my wife was dead, I think that I would still have given myself, undisturbed by that knowledge, to the contemplation of her image, and that my mental conversation with her would have been just as vivid and satisfying.

The wedding of Tilly Grosser, 1941.
Source: Viktor Frankl Institute, Vienna, Austria.

COLLEAGUE: Just as vivid.

FRANKL: Yes. As it is said, "Set me like a seal upon thy heart, love is as strong as death."

End of Scene 10

Scene 11

The Inner Life of the Prisoner

Title Board:	**THE INNER LIFE OF THE PRISONER**
	Sunsets are free
	Colleague; Frankl; Guard
Visual:	Camp photo. Sunset superimposed over camp. Digging. Photo of Tilly Frankl.
Stage Directions:	Start with photo of the inside of a hut. Then the outside. Then a sunset. Digging. End up with photo of Tilly Frankl.

COLLEAGUE: You had only your thoughts, your inner thoughts, through that long time. Tell me about that.

FRANKL: Yes, the inner life. As it became more intense for each prisoner, he also experienced the beauty of art and nature as never before. Under their influence he sometimes even forgot his own frightful circumstances.

COLLEAGUE: Give me an example.

FRANKL: Yes. Yes. You know, if someone had seen our faces on the journey from Auschwitz to a Bavarian camp as we beheld the mountains of Salzburg with their summits glowing in the sunset, through the little barred windows of the prison carriage, he would never have believed that those were the faces of men who had given up all hope of life and liberty. Despite that factor—or maybe because of it—we were carried away by nature's beauty.

COLLEAGUE: Can you give me some more examples?

FRANKL: In camp a man might draw the attention of a comrade to a nice view of the setting sun shining through the tall trees of the Bavarian woods.

COLLEAGUE: As in that famous watercolor by Dürer.

FRANKL: Yes. I even recall one remarkable evening when we were already resting dead tired on the floor of our hut, soup bowls in hand, when a fellow prisoner rushed in and asked us outside to see the wonderful sunset.

COLLEAGUE: And you all went?

FRANKL: Those who could, to see sinister clouds glowing in the west, and the whole sky alive with clouds of ever-changing shapes and colors, from steel blue to blood red. The desolate gray mud huts provided a sharp contrast, while the puddles on the muddy ground reflected the glowing sky. Then, then, after minutes of moving silence, one prisoner said, "How beautiful the world *could* be!"

COLLEAGUE: Could be. Could be. And you continued your inner life, the conversations with your wife?

FRANKL: Of course. There was another day we were at work in a trench. I was again conversing silently with my wife, or perhaps I was struggling to find the *reason* for my sufferings.

COLLEAGUE: You were struggling with your slow dying.

FRANKL: Then, in a last violent protest against the hopelessness of my imminent death, I sensed my spirit soaring outwards. It transcended that hopeless, meaningless world, and

Viktor Frankl in his office clinic, 1985.

from somewhere I heard a victorious "Yes" in answer to my question.

COLLEAGUE: The question of the existence of an ultimate purpose.

FRANKL: And at that moment, that very moment, a light was lit in a distant farmhouse, in the midst of a miserable gray of a dawn in Bavaria—"The light shineth in the darkness."

COLLEAGUE: *"Et lux in tenebris lucet."*

GUARD: Stop dreaming. Work. Dig, you lazy piece of shit.

FRANKL: Once again I communed with my wife. She was with me. I had the feeling that I was able to touch her. The feeling was very strong: she was *there*. Then, at that very moment, a bird flew down silently and perched just in front of me, on the heap of soil I had just dug, and looked steadily at me.

COLLEAGUE: Who was that bird?

Fences.
Source: Hartmann, E. (1995). In the Camps.

End of Scene 11

Psychological Factors in the Camps

Title Board:	**PSYCHOLOGICAL FACTORS IN THE CAMPS**
	Suffering and Eternal Life
	Colleague; Frankl; Man; Woman
Visual:	Woman in camp clothes, view of tree branch through a window.
Stage Directions:	Sounds of wind in trees, running water, birdsong.

COLLEAGUE: You're a psychiatrist. You must have been studying yourself and the prisoners and your keepers all of the time. What did you learn?

FRANKL: Apathy was endemic—epidemic might be a better word. The majority of the prisoners suffered from a kind of inferiority complex. On the outside we fancied ourselves as "somebody"; here we were treated like complete nonentities.

COLLEAGUE: What about the special prisoners, the ones you called "prominent"? You know, the Capos, the cooks, the storekeepers, and the camp policemen.

FRANKL: They didn't feel degraded at all—on the contrary, promoted! What do you think of that Capo?

MAN: Imagine! I knew that man when he was only a bank president. Isn't it fortunate that he has risen so far in the world?

COLLEAGUE: Is everything relative?

FRANKL: Yes and no. Survival is an absolute. We always have choice of action, if not external, then internal. Man can preserve a vestige of spiritual freedom, of independence of mind.

COLLEAGUE: Even in those camps?

FRANKL: Yes. We who lived there can remember men who comforted others, gave away their last piece of bread.

COLLEAGUE: Not many!

FRANKL: Enough. Enough. They may have been very few in number, but they offer sufficient proof that everything can be taken from a man but one thing: the last of the human freedoms—to choose one's attitude in any given set of circumstances, to choose one's own way.

COLLEAGUE: As you did.

FRANKL: To survive as a human being. Every day had opportunities to make a decision which determined whether or not you would submit to those powers which threatened to rob you of your very self, your inner freedom. Any man can decide what shall become of him—mentally and spiritually.

COLLEAGUE: Wasn't it Dostoyevsky who said, "There is only one thing that I dread: not to be worthy of my sufferings"?

FRANKL: Yes. Those words came to me often, especially about those martyrs in the camp whose suffering and death bore witness to the fact that the last inner freedom cannot be lost—the way they bore their suffering was a genuine inner achievement.

COLLEAGUE: Is such suffering necessary?

FRANKL: If there is meaning in life at all, then there must be a meaning in suffering. Suffering is an ineradicable part of life, even as fate and death. Without suffering and death human life cannot be complete.

COLLEAGUE: Again I ask, is suffering necessary?

FRANKL: No. It is not necessary. Yet, there are often circumstances beyond our control—the camps, accidents, diseases—that happen. The way in which a man accepts his fate—those things beyond his control—can add a deeper meaning to his life. He controls how he responds.

COLLEAGUE: Few can do that.

FRANKL: Of the prisoners, it is true that only a few kept their full inner liberty and attained these values, but even one such example is sufficient proof that man's inner strength may raise him above his outward fate. And such men are not only in concentration camps—those opportunities are every-where. Let me tell you a story.

COLLEAGUE: I'm listening!

FRANKL: I met a young woman in the camps who knew that she would die in the next few days.

Two survivors in Bergen-Belsen, April 30, 1945.
Source: Zelizer, B. (2000). Visual Culture and The Holocaust.

WOMAN: I am grateful that fate has hit me so hard. In my former life I was spoiled and did not take spiritual accomplishments seriously.

FRANKL: Yes.

WOMAN: This tree here out my window is the only friend I have in my loneliness. I can see just one branch of that chestnut tree— on that branch are two blossoms. Do you see, too?

FRANKL: Yes.

WOMAN: I often talk to this tree.

FRANKL: Does the tree reply?

WOMAN: Yes.

FRANKL: What does it say?

WOMAN: I am here—I am here—I am life, eternal life.

The Wailing Wall, 1988.

End of Scene 12

Scene 13

Being a Typhus Doctor and Acting Like a Sheep

Title Board:	**BEING A TYPHUS DOCTOR**
	Acting like a sheep
	Colleague; Frankl
Visual:	Doctor examining a patient. Sheep and crowds of prisoners. Corpses. Tilly Frankl.
Stage Directions:	When showing sheep and crowds of prisoners, add low level of sheepdogs barking. Have photo of Tilly Frankl at end—start out sharp and then lose focus as light fades.

COLLEAGUE: You did work as a doctor sometimes, didn't you?

FRANKL: I was on my fourth day in the sick quarters when the chief doctor rushed in and asked me to volunteer for medical duties in another camp containing typhus patients. Against the urgent advice of my friends, I decided to volunteer. You see, I knew that in a working party I would die in a short time. But, if I had to die, there might at least be some sense in my death. For me, this was simple mathematics, not sacrifice.

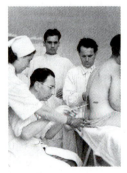

COLLEAGUE: Very fortunate, and very realistic.

Lumbar puncture, 1940.

FRANKL: More than you can imagine, for secretly the warrant officer had ordered that the two doctors who had

Source: Viktor Frankl Institute, Vienna, Austria.

53

volunteered should "be taken care of" till they left. We looked so weak that he feared we might die.

COLLEAGUE: Another strange miracle on your path to survival.

FRANKL: Those odd circumstances, and acting like a sheep.

COLLEAGUE: Like a sheep?

FRANKL: Yes, of course. We were herded everywhere. Safety was not only being in the flock, but the center of the flock. There, the bad dogs and the herders could not get at you. One of the camp's most imperative survival laws was: Do not be conspicuous—we tried at all times to avoid the attention of the SS.

COLLEAGUE: Still, there must have been a great craving for some solitude, to be alone with your thoughts.

FRANKL: After my transportation to a so-called "rest camp," I had the rare fortune to find solitude for about five minutes at a time. Behind the earthen hut where I worked, and in which were crowded about fifty delirious patients, there was a quiet spot in the corner of the double fence of barbed wire. A tent sheltered the half-dozen daily corpses.

COLLEAGUE: A bad place.

FRANKL: Corpses, I was used to. But there was also a wooden lid over a shaft leading to the water pipes. Whenever I could steal a few minutes, I squatted on this lid and looked out at the green flowering slopes and distant hills of the Bavarian landscape. I dreamed longingly.

COLLEAGUE: But not for long.

FRANKL: A passing guard or my duties called me back. The medical supply might be five to ten aspirins, which we only used for those who still had some hope. For the light cases, all I could do was give some words of encouragement.

COLLEAGUE: You practiced your own form of triage.

FRANKL: There was no choice. Medicine would not have helped the desperately ill.

COLLEAGUE: Life had little value there.

FRANKL: The camp inmate was hardened. For example, when a convoy of sick men was arranged, it was only the number that counted—if a man died before the cart left, his body was thrown on to the cart to keep the number correct! The list was the only thing that mattered.

COLLEAGUE: Their records had to be correct.

FRANKL: The prisoners had to use every means to improve their chances of survival. They were not sentimental, but also completely dependent on the *moods* of the guards—mere playthings of fate.

A British soldier clearing corpses at Bergen-Belsen.
Source: Zelizer, B. (2000). Visual Culture and The Holocaust.

COLLEAGUE: Yet, within those random events, something, perhaps someone, took care of you.

FRANKL: I had learned to let fate take its course. I stayed with the transfer to the "rest camp" even though my friends told me it would be my death. It wasn't. They even reverted to cannibalism in that camp after I left—it got so bad.

COLLEAGUE: You were not afraid.

FRANKL: I was always afraid. I even made my friend Otto memorize my will in case he survived and I didn't.

COLLEAGUE: Do you remember that will?

FRANKL: I said, "Listen, Otto, if I don't get back home to my wife, and if you should see her again, then tell her that I talked of her hourly, daily. You remember. Secondly, I have loved her more than anyone. Thirdly, the short time I have been married to her outweighs everything, even all we have gone through here."

COLLEAGUE: And, Otto?

FRANKL: I never saw him again. Or my wife. Or my wife.

End of Scene 13

Scene 14

The Science Teacher

Title Board:	**THE SCIENCE TEACHER**
	Oxidationalism
	Science Teacher; Frankl; Colleague
Visual:	Classroom, molecules, picture of thirteen-year-old Frankl.
Stage Directions:	Use slides to illustrate this vignette.

Frankl's family, 1925. Source: Viktor Frankl Institute, Vienna, Austria.

SCIENCE TEACHER: I must emphasize the findings of science. You see, life in the final analysis is nothing but a combustion process, an oxidation process.

FRANKL: [*Jumping to his feet.*] Professor Fritz, if this be the case, what meaning does life have?

COLLEAGUE: He had no answer?

FRANKL: He could not answer because he was a reductionist.

COLLEAGUE: Really?

FRANKL: To be sure, in his case one has not really to deal with an example of reductionism, but ironically with an instance of what he would call "oxidationalism"!

[*Pause.*]

SCIENCE TEACHER: I must emphasize the findings of science. You see, life in the final analysis is nothing but a combustion process, an oxidation process.

Frankl with hiking friends in the 1930s.
Source: Viktor Frankl Institute, Vienna, Austria.

FRANKL: [*Jumping to his feet.*] Professor Fritz, if this be the case, what meaning does life have?

COLLEAGUE: He had no answer?

FRANKL: He could not answer because he was a reductionist.

End of Scene 14

Act II

Scene 15

The Size of Human Suffering

Title Board:	**THE SIZE OF HUMAN SUFFERING**
	De-lousing. No chimney!
	Frankl; Colleague
Visual:	Standing outside in the rain. Camp crematorium. Three photos showing delousing behind a back-lit sheet. Ladling soup.
Stage Directions:	Match visuals to dialogue. Delousing via a series of slides.

FRANKL: A man's suffering is similar to the behavior of a gas which will completely fill any size of empty container. Suffering completely fills the human soul and conscious mind. Therefore, the "size" of human suffering is absolutely relative.

Crematorium.
Source: Hartmann, E. (1995). In the Camps.

COLLEAGUE: From the loss of a favorite pet to that of a loved one.

FRANKL: Yes. It follows that a very trifling thing can cause the greatest of joys. We were being moved from Auschwitz and were all afraid that the destination was the Mauthausen camp. You cannot possibly imagine the dance of joy performed in the carriage by the prisoners when we realized we were "only" heading for Dachau!

COLLEAGUE: Only Dachau!

FRANKL: When we arrived the first important news was that this comparatively small camp—only two thousand five hundred—had no "oven," no crematorium, no gas! A person who became a "Moslem" would have to wait to be returned to Auschwitz to be killed. We laughed and cracked jokes.

COLLEAGUE: It was not all jokes.

FRANKL: One of our members was missing and we had to stand all night and into the next morning, outside, frozen and soaked to the skin. Yet we were all very pleased—no chimney!

COLLEAGUE: It was all relative.

FRANKL: We envied convicts who had it much better than us. We longed for a factory job in a sheltered room. All of the outside work parties were different. Some foremen maintained a tradition of dealing out numerous blows. I was once in such a group and was saved by an air-raid alarm which made it necessary to regroup the workers.

COLLEAGUE: You were saved by many such strange happenings.

FRANKL: We were grateful for the smallest of mercies like enough time to delouse before going to bed.

COLLEAGUE: How was that done?

FRANKL: It meant standing naked in an unheated hut where icicles hung from the ceiling. If there were no air-raid alarm, we had

Janina Tollik: "Punishment Parade" (Oil). Source: Poznanski, S. (1963). Struggle, Death, Memory. 1939–1945.

light for this. Otherwise, we were kept awake half the night by the lice.

COLLEAGUE: Tell me more.

FRANKL: A small thing, but it was a cherished pleasure. There was one prisoner-cook who dealt out the soup equally—a remarkable thing. I was in his line for a while.

COLLEAGUE: He didn't help his friends.

FRANKL: True. But it is not for me to pass judgment on those who did. No man should judge unless he asks himself in absolute honesty whether in a similar situation he might not have done the same.

COLLEAGUE: You mean, who can question a man who favors his friends when sooner or later it is a question of life and death?

FRANKL: Yes.

End of Scene 15

Scene 16

Art in a Concentration Camp

Title Board:	**ART IN A CONCENTRATION CAMP?**
	Theater and music
	Colleague; Frankl
Visual:	Photo of camp entertainment: someone singing, doing stand-up comedy, playing a violin, reciting, soup tureen on a well-laid-out table in color in a home.
Stage Directions:	Match visuals to dialogue, ending with a modern table setting with a soup tureen. Underscore with sounds of singing, laughter, monologue, violin.

COLLEAGUE: Is there such a thing as art in a concentration camp?

FRANKL: A kind of cabaret was improvised from time to time.

COLLEAGUE: Where?

FRANKL: A hut was cleared temporarily. Some benches were pushed or nailed together and a program drawn up.

COLLEAGUE: Who came?

FRANKL: Those who had good positions in the camp: Capos and the workers who did not have to leave camp on distant marches. They came together to laugh or cry, anyway, to forget.

COLLEAGUE: Who performed?

FRANKL: Anyone who wanted to. There were songs, poems, jokes, some with underlying satire regarding the camp. They helped us forget and were so effective that many ordinary prisoners attended even though they were fatigued or missed a meal.

COLLEAGUE: Quite remarkable.

FRANKL: At our half-hour lunch breaks with soup provided by the contractor there was sometimes a special treat.

COLLEAGUE: Other than the thin watery soup?

FRANKL: There was a prisoner who climbed on a tub and sang Italian arias. We enjoyed the songs, and he was guaranteed a double helping of soup, straight "from the bottom"—that meant with peas!

COLLEAGUE: So there were short times when music was in your lives. In such a setting!

FRANKL: Generally speaking, any pursuit of art in camp was somewhat grotesque. But you might be even more astonished to learn that one could find a sense of humor there as well. Humor was another of the soul's weapons in the fight for self-preservation.

COLLEAGUE: Humor in that place? Can you give me an example?

FRANKL: I practically trained a friend to develop a sense of humor. I suggested to him that we would promise each other to invent at least one amusing story daily, but this story had to be about some incident that could happen after our liberation.

COLLEAGUE: Yes.

FRANKL: One such was a future dinner engagement when he would forget himself when the soup was served, and beg the hostess to ladle it "from the bottom"!

End of Scene 16

Scene 17

Decisions and Escape

Title Board:	MAKING DECISIONS
	Escaping?
	Colleague; Frankl; Man
Visual:	Camp, fences, world seen through fences, trucks driving out of camp, Red Cross car, a beat-up rucksack, three corpses.
Stage Directions:	Coordinate slides and dialogue. Some birdsong in the background. Car and truck noises.

COLLEAGUE: Did you ever try to escape?

FRANKL: That's an interesting question. You see, the camp inmate was frightened of making decisions and of taking any sort of initiative whatsoever.

Camp.
Source: Frankl, V.E. (1997). Viktor Frankl Recollections. An Autobiography.

Camp Wire.
Source: Hartmann, E. (1995). In the Camps.

COLLEAGUE: Why was that?

FRANKL: Well, this was the result of a strong feeling that fate was one's master, and that one must not try to influence it in any way. In addition, there was a great apathy.

COLLEAGUE: But you still thought of escape?

FRANKL: Yes. The decision had to be a lightning one. Great torments assailed the inmate—should he take the risk?

COLLEAGUE: And?

FRANKL: As the battle front grew nearer, a colleague of mine invited me to join him for a pretended consultation outside the fence. This patient needed a specialist's advice.

COLLEAGUE: But you didn't escape then.

FRANKL: The resistance fighter never showed up and there were some other difficulties. We had to return to the camp.

COLLEAGUE: Were you disappointed?

FRANKL: Yes and no. This gave us an opportunity to break into an empty hut in the women's camp. My friend found a rucksack. There were other items. Bowls were very useful, but we couldn't tell whether they had been used as toilets.

COLLEAGUE: You were still thinking of escape.

FRANKL: Of course. So I ran back to my hut to collect all my possessions: my food bowl, a pair of torn mittens "inherited" from a dead typhus patient, and a few scraps of shorthand notes for my book. I made a last quick round of my patients and came to my only countryman, who was almost dying. It was my ambition to save his life.

MAN: You, too, are getting out doctor?

FRANKL: No. No. I just need to check the other patients.

MAN: I understand.

FRANKL: He gave me such a hopeless look. Suddenly, I decided to take fate in my own hands for once. I had an unhappy feeling.

COLLEAGUE: What did you do?

FRANKL: I ran out of the hut and told my friend I could not go with him. As soon as I told him with finality that I had made up my mind to stay with my patients, the unhappy feeling left me. I did not know what the following days would bring, but I had gained an inward peace that I had never experienced before.

MAN: Thank you for staying and being with me.

FRANKL: Thank you, my friend.

COLLEAGUE: You were now close to liberation.

FRANKL: Our last day in camp arrived. Mass transports had taken nearly all the prisoners to other camps, and the Capos and cooks had fled. We got orders to evacuate completely by sun-set, and then they closed the gates, locking us in. My friend and I were to bury three men outside the barbed wire—we were the only two in the camp who had strength enough to do the job.

COLLEAGUE: You had a plan?

FRANKL: With the first body we would smuggle out the rucksack in the old laundry tub that served as a coffin. With the second body we would take out my rucksack. On the third trip we would escape. After the second trip I waited and waited for my friend to come back with a scrap of bread. But we did not get that far.

COLLEAGUE: What happened?

FRANKL: At the very moment my friend came back, the camp gates were thrown open. A delegate from the International Red Cross in Geneva had arrived in a splendid aluminum-colored car, painted with large red crosses. We were now under his protection.

COLLEAGUE: No more need to escape!

FRANKL: Boxes of medicine were unloaded from the car, cigarettes were distributed, we were photographed, and joy reigned supreme.

U.S. forces at Ohrdruf concentration camp. General Eisenhower can be seen in the front row, third from the left. Photo by Harold Royall.
Source: Zelizer, B. (2000). Visual Culture and The Holocaust.

COLLEAGUE: What about the third body?

FRANKL: We buried that now in the shallow grave with the other two. The guard even joined us in our short prayers. The words of our prayer asking for peace were as fervent as any ever uttered by the human voice.

COLLEAGUE: So, you were now free.

FRANKL: No. We had rejoiced too early. That night the SS arrived with trucks and an order to clear the camp. We were to be taken to a central camp and then to Switzerland to exchange for some prisoners of war.

COLLEAGUE: But you didn't go!

FRANKL: Let me finish. The SS were strange—they were so friendly, persuading us to get in the trucks without fear. We openly had our rucksacks with us. At the last truck, the chief doctor left us out, and we had to stay behind.

COLLEAGUE: Fate again.

Corpses.
Source: Frankl, V.E. (1997). Viktor Frankl Recollections.
An Autobiography.

FRANKL: We waited a long time. The next morning there was gun-
fire. The battle front had reached us. Outside the camp gate
was a white flag on a pole. Fate was certainly with us. Our
friends in the trucks were taken to a small camp nearby, locked
into huts, and burned to death. Why was I saved again?

End of Scene 17

Scene 18

Faith in the Future

Title Board:	**FAITH IN THE FUTURE—HOPE AND …**
	Frankl speaks in the hut
	Colleague; Frankl
Visual:	Camp scenes, suicide on the wire. Slide stating, "It did not really matter what we expected from life, but rather what life expected from us." Another slide stating, "That which does not kill me, makes me stronger—Nietzsche."
Stage Directions:	Integrate visuals with dialogue, especially the two quotes.

COLLEAGUE: You were living in the moment, in the present all of the time. What was time like for you?

FRANKL: Our time sense was distorted. In camp a day filled with its hourly tortures and fatigue appeared endless. A larger time unit, perhaps a week, seemed to pass very quickly. My comrades agreed when I said that in camp a day lasted longer than a week.

COLLEAGUE: What about the future?

FRANKL: Let me tell you a story about the day when I was almost in tears from the pain from the sores on my feet. I limped a few kilometers in a cold bitter wind. My thoughts circulated on the endless little problems of our miserable life.

COLLEAGUE: You were obsessed with the trivia of survival.

FRANKL: I became disgusted and forced myself to turn to another subject.

COLLEAGUE: Yes?

FRANKL: Suddenly, I saw myself standing on the platform of a well-lit, warm, and pleasant lecture room. In front of me sat an attentive audience on comfortable upholstered seats. I was giving a lecture on the psychology of the concentration camp!

COLLEAGUE: A daydream that became a reality.

FRANKL: All that oppressed me at that moment became objective, seen and described from the remote viewpoint of science. By this method I succeeded somehow in rising above the situation, above the sufferings of the moment, and I observed them as if they were already in the past.

COLLEAGUE: Dissociation under stress is not uncommon.

FRANKL: Don't trivialize. This was real. Both I and my troubles became the object of an interesting psychoscientific study undertaken by myself. Did not Spinoza say, "Emotion, which is suffering, ceases to be suffering as soon as we form a clear and precise picture of it"?

COLLEAGUE: You transcended the moment.

FRANKL: You see, the prisoner who lost faith in the future—his future—was doomed. With his loss of belief in the future, he also lost his spiritual hold.

COLLEAGUE: This became a veritable death sentence.

FRANKL: And it came on very quickly. We feared these well-known symptoms in our friends. No entreaties had any effect after this crisis. They simply gave up.

COLLEAGUE: Wasn't there a sudden increase in the death rate?

FRANKL: The week between Christmas 1944 and New Year's 1945 showed an exceptional death rate. The majority of prisoners had lived in the naïve hope that they would be home again by

Christmas. As the time grew near with no encouraging news, they lost courage, their resistance decreased, and they died.

COLLEAGUE: The incredible power of hope and hopelessness.

FRANKL: Nietzsche's words were prophetic: "He who has a *why* to live for can bear with almost any *how*." Woe to him who saw no more sense in his life, no aim, no purpose, no point in carrying on.

COLLEAGUE: He was soon lost.

FRANKL: We had to learn ourselves and we had to teach the despairing men, that *it did not really matter what we expected from life, but rather what life expected from us.*

COLLEAGUE: You had to stop asking about the meaning of life, but instead think of yourselves as those being questioned by life—moment by moment.

FRANKL: Life ultimately means taking the responsibility to find the right answer to its problems, and to fulfill the different tasks which it constantly sets for each individual.

COLLEAGUE: Every situation is distinguished by its uniqueness.

FRANKL: When a man finds it is his destiny to suffer, he will have to accept his suffering as his single and unique task. We had to realize the hidden opportunities of this suffering.

COLLEAGUE: All of that suffering, and especially the hopelessness, the being out of control, must have led to a lot of suicide as a means of escape. I mean, this was an act under their control.

FRANKL: There was a very strict camp ruling that forbade any efforts to save a man who attempted suicide. It was forbidden, for example, to cut down a man who was trying to hang himself.

COLLEAGUE: Less work for the guards.

FRANKL: You see, our efforts were to prevent the suicide from occurring.

COLLEAGUE: How did you do that?

FRANKL: I can think of two cases of would-be suicide. Both men talked about their intentions. It was a question of getting them to realize that life was still expecting something of them.

COLLEAGUE: You mean, something in their future was expected of them.

FRANKL: Yes. For one we found that it was his child, whom he adored, and who was waiting for him in a foreign country. For the other it was a thing, not a person. He was a scientist who still needed to complete a series of books—and no one else could do this work.

COLLEAGUE: Dreams and visions.

FRANKL: We are all unique. When the impossibility of replacing a person is realized, it allows the responsibility which a man has for his existence and its continuance to appear in all its magnitude. Once a man realizes that, he cannot throw his life away.

COLLEAGUE: So you struggled on.

FRANKL: One day, we, all two thousand five hundred of us, had chosen a day of fasting rather than give up a man who had stolen a few pounds of potatoes. On the evening of the day of fasting we lay in our earthen huts— in a very low mood. To make matters even

Camp Wire.
Source: Hartmann, E. (1995).
In the Camps.

worse, the light went out. But our senior block warden was a wise man. He improvised a little talk. He talked about the many comrades who had died in the past few days, either of sickness or of suicide. He also mentioned what may have been the real reason for their deaths: giving up hope. Then he asked me to speak, to give some advice about preventing possible future victims from reaching this extreme state. I was very tired, yet I spoke of the present—things could be worse, yet we had lost little that was irretrievable. We could rebuild health, happiness, family, professional abilities, fortune, position in society. After all, we still had our bones intact. I quoted from Nietzsche, "*Was mich nicht umbringt, Macht mich starker.*"

COLLEAGUE: That which does not kill me, makes me stronger.

FRANKL: Then I spoke of the future. Since there was no typhus epidemic in the camp, I estimated my own chances at about one in twenty. In spite of this I did not give up hope—for no man knew what the future would bring.

COLLEAGUE: The future is hope.

FRANKL: I also mentioned the past—all of its joys, how its light ever shone in the present darkness. I quoted the poet, "*Was du erlebst, kann keine Macht der Welt dir rauben.*"

COLLEAGUE: What you have experienced, no power on earth can take from you.

FRANKL: There is so much that we had already brought into being, and having been is also a kind of being, perhaps the surest kind.

COLLEAGUE: You were yourself transformed that evening.

FRANKL: Then I spoke of the many opportunities of giving life a meaning. Human life, under any circumstances, never ceases to have a meaning.

COLLEAGUE: And that infinite meaning of life includes suffering and dying, privation and death.

FRANKL: For each of us. I said that someone looks down on us in our difficult hours—a friend, a wife, somebody alive or dead, or a God—and he would not expect us to disappoint him.

COLLEAGUE: You would know how to suffer proudly.

FRANKL: Finally, I spoke of our sacrifice, which had meaning in every case, in every case. It was the nature of this sacrifice that it should appear pointless in the normal world, but in reality our sacrifice did have a meaning.

COLLEAGUE: How did they respond?

FRANKL: When the light flared up again, I saw the miserable figures of my friends limping towards me to thank me with tears in their eyes.

COLLEAGUE: You succeeded then.

FRANKL: But I have to confess here that only too rarely had I the inner strength to make contact with my companions in suffering, and that I missed many opportunities to do so.

End of Scene 18

Scene 19

After Liberation

Title Board:	**THE GUARDS**
	After liberation
	Colleague; Frankl; Man
Visual:	Two or three guard photos, open gates, clouds, fields, released prisoners eating and sitting.
Stage Directions:	Black-and-white photos yielding to colored ones of meadows and forests and clouds.

COLLEAGUE: Before you speak about the psychology of the prisoners after the liberation, what about the camp guards? How could they do what they did?

FRANKL: First, among the guards there were some sadists, sadists in the pure clinical sense. Second, these sadists were always selected when a really severe detachment of guards was needed. Third, the feelings of the majority of guards had been dulled by the number of years in which, in ever-increasing doses, they had witnessed the brutal methods of the camp.

COLLEAGUE: Yet some of those men refused to take an active part in sadistic measures.

FRANKL: True. But they did not prevent others.

COLLEAGUE: A small sop to their consciences.

FRANKL: Fourth, it must be stated that even among the guards there were some who took pity on us. We found out after liberation that my last camp commander paid out of his own pocket for medicines for prisoners. But the senior camp

warden, a prisoner himself, was harder than any SS guard—
he beat other prisoners at every slightest opportunity.

COLLEAGUE: You just couldn't tell.

FRANKL: Human kindness can be found in all groups. I remember
how one day a foreman secretly gave me a piece of bread—
he must have saved this from his breakfast ration. It was far
more than the small piece of bread which moved me to tears
at the time. It was the human "something" which this man
also gave to me—the word and look which accompanied the
gift.

COLLEAGUE: So, the prisoners were profoundly moved by the
smallest kindness received from any of the guards.

FRANKL: You know, from all this we may learn that there are two
races of men in this world, but only these two—the "race" of
the decent man, and the "race" of the indecent man. Both are
found everywhere. No group is of "pure race," and therefore
one occasionally found a decent fellow among camp guards.

COLLEAGUE: Only occasionally, only occasionally.

FRANKL: Life in a concentration camp tore open the human soul
and exposed its depths. Is it surprising that in those depths
we again found human qualities which in their very nature
were a mixture of good and evil?

COLLEAGUE: And after the liberation?

FRANKL: On that day there was a sense of total relaxation. But it
would be wrong to think that we went mad with joy.

COLLEAGUE: What then? Some kind of anticlimax?

FRANKL: With tired steps we dragged ourselves to the camp gates,
looking timidly around. Then we ventured a few steps out of
camp. No orders were shouted at us! No blows or kicks! Oh,
no! This time the guards offered us cigarettes! We walked
slowly along the road leading from the camp—we wanted to

see the camp's surroundings with the eyes of free men. "Freedom"—we repeated to ourselves, and yet we could not grasp it.

COLLEAGUE: You had dreamed about it so much that perhaps it had lost its meaning.

FRANKL: We could not grasp the fact that freedom was ours. We came to a meadow full of flowers. We saw and realized that they were there, but we had no feelings about them. The first spark of joy came when we saw a rooster with a tail of multi-colored feathers—but it remained only a spark.

COLLEAGUE: When did you really know?

FRANKL: In the evening when we all met again in our hut, one said secretly to the other—

MAN: Tell me, were you pleased today?

FRANKL: We replied, "Truthfully, no!" We had literally lost the ability to feel pleased, and had to relearn it slowly.

COLLEAGUE: In some ways that was a more brutal act than the beatings and the killings.

FRANKL: In psychological terms, the liberated prisoners were depersonalized—everything appeared unreal, unlikely, as in a dream.

COLLEAGUE: Yet dreams end and you wake up.

FRANKL: You don't understand—we didn't believe that. How often had we been deceived by our dreams to wake to a shrill whistle?

COLLEAGUE: But now the dream had really come true.

FRANKL: But could we truly believe in it? Could we?

COLLEAGUE: Slowly, yes, reality must win out.

FRANKL: Our bodies believed it first. We, our bodies, ate ravenously, for hours and days, even half the night.

COLLEAGUE: You were amazed, I'm sure, as to how much you could eat.

FRANKL: It took days. For me it was a few days after liberation when I walked through the country, past flowering meadows, for miles and miles. Larks rose to the sky and I could hear their joyous song. There was no one around, just the wide earth and sky and the larks' jubilation and the freedom of space.

COLLEAGUE: The freedom of space.

FRANKL: At that moment, I stopped and looked around and fell to my knees. One sentence came to my mind over and over: "I called to the Lord from my narrow prison and He answered me in the freedom of space."

COLLEAGUE: The freedom of space.

FRANKL: How long I knelt there and repeated that sentence I can no longer recall. But I know that on that day, in that hour, my new life started. Step for step I progressed, until I again became a human being.

End of Scene 19

Scene 20

Dr J.'s Story

Title Board: **DR J.'S STORY**

A truly satanic being?

Colleague; Frankl

Visual: Hospital in Vienna, Hitler rallies in Vienna, Ljubjanka prison in Moscow, Nazi medical doctors.

Stage Directions: Integrate slides with the text.

Frankl and the hospital team. Source: Viktor Frankl Institute, Vienna, Austria.

COLLEAGUE: You mentioned a Dr J. Can you tell me his story?

FRANKL: Let me cite the following case. It concerns Dr J., the only man I have ever encountered in my whole life whom I would dare to characterize as a satanic being. At the time I knew of him, he was generally called "The mass murderer of Steinhof," the name of the large mental hospital in Vienna. When the Nazis had started their euthanasia program, he held all the strings in his hands and was so fanatic in the job assigned to him that he tried not to let one single psychotic individual escape the gas chamber. The few patients who did escape were, paradoxically, Jews. It happened that a small ward in a Jewish home for aging people remained unknown to Dr J.; and, though the Gestapo which supervised this institution had strictly forbidden the admission of any psychotic

83

Hitler Wien.
Source: Frankl, V.E. (1997). Viktor Frankl
Recollections. An Autobiography.

patients, I succeeded in smuggling in and hiding such patients
there by issuing false diagnostic certificates. I manipulated
the symptomology in these cases so as to indicate aphasia
instead of schizophrenia. I also administered illegal metrazol
shocks. Thus these Jewish patients could be rescued, whereas
even the relatives of Nazi party functionaries were "mercy"-
killed. When I came back to Vienna—after having myself
escaped from being sent to the gas chamber in Auschwitz—I
asked what happened to Dr J. "He had been imprisoned by
the Russians in one of the isolation cells of Steinhof," they
told me. "The next day, however, the door of his cell stood
open and Dr J. was never seen again." Later, I was convinced
that, like others, he had by the help of his comrades found his
way to South America. More recently, however, I was con-
sulted by a former high-ranking Austrian diplomat who had
been imprisoned behind the Iron Curtain for many years, first
in Siberia, and then in the famous Ljubjanka prison in
Moscow. While I was examining him neurologically, he suddenly asked me whether I happened to know Dr J. After my
affirmative reply he continued: "I made his acquaintance in
Ljubjanka. There he died, at about forty, from cancer of the
urinary bladder. Before he died, however, he showed himself
to be the best comrade you can imagine! He gave consolation

to everybody. He lived up to the highest conceivable moral standard. He was the best friend I ever met during my long years in prison!"

This is the story of Dr J., "the mass murderer of Steinhof." How can you dare to predict the behavior of man! What you may predict are the movements of a machine, of an apparatus, of an automaton. More than that, you may even try to predict the mechanisms or "dynamisms" of the human psyche as well; but man is more than psyche: Man is spirit. By the very act of his own self-transcendence he leaves the plane of the merely biopsychological and enters the sphere of the specifically human, the noölogical dimension. Human existence is, in its essence, noëtic. A human being is not one thing among others: things are determining each other, but man is self-determining. In actuality, man is free and responsible, and these constituents of his

Young Frankl at the clinic, 1930.
Source: Viktor Frankl Institute, Vienna, Austria.

spirituality, i.e., freedom and responsibility, must never be clouded by what is called the reification or depersonalization of man.

End of Scene 20

Scene 21

Some Personal Stories

Title Board:	**SOME PERSONAL STORIES**
	Family
	Elly-Frau Frankl
	Colleague; Frankl; Frankl's Father
Visual:	Frankl's parents, Frankl with brother and sister, Frankl family, mountaineering, Elly, Gabriele and Franz, grandchildren, with Pope Paul VI.
Stage Directions:	Integrate family photos with text.

Frankl as a child.
Source: Viktor Frankl Institute, Vienna, Austria.

COLLEAGUE: When were you born?

FRANKL: I was born in Vienna on March 26, 1905. My birthday coincides with the day Beethoven died.

COLLEAGUE: You had some famous ancestors.

FRANKL: My mother was a descendant of an old and established Prague patrician family. Among her ancestors was Rashi, who lived in the twelfth century, and "Maharal," the "High Rabbi

Löw" of Prague who was made famous in the novel *The Golem*.

COLLEAGUE: Your mother blessed you before you were all deported to Auschwitz.

FRANKL: When the time had come and I was to be deported to the Auschwitz death camp with my first wife, Tilly, I said farewell to my dear mother. At that last moment I asked Mother, "Please give me your blessing." I can never forget how she cried out, from deep within her heart, "Yes! Yes, I bless you!"—and then she gave me her blessing. This was only a week before she herself was deported to Auschwitz and sent directly to the gas chamber.

Viktor Frankl's parents, 1901.
Source: Viktor Frankl Institute, Vienna, Austria.

COLLEAGUE: And the last time you saw your father …

FRANKL: Among the few things I was able to smuggle into Theresienstadt was a vial of morphine. When my father was dying from pulmonary edema, and struggling for air as he neared death, I injected him with the morphine to ease his suffering. He was then eighty-one years old and starving. Nevertheless, it took a second pneumonia to bring about his death.

I asked him, "Do you still have pain?"

FRANKL'S FATHER: No.

FRANKL: Do you have any wish?

FRANKL'S FATHER: No.

FRANKL: Do you want to tell me anything?

The Frankl family, 1925. From left to right: Viktor, Gabriel, Elsa, Stella, and Walter.
Source: Frankl, V.E. (1997). Viktor Frankl Recollections. An Autobiography.

FRANKL'S FATHER: No.

FRANKL: I kissed him and left. I knew I would not see him alive again. But I had the most wonderful feeling one can imagine. I had done what I could. I had stayed in Vienna because of my parents, and now I had accompanied Father to the threshold and had spared him the unnecessary agony of death.

COLLEAGUE: Your thoughts on their deaths and death?

FRANKL: In some respects it is death itself that makes life meaningful. Most importantly, the transitoriness of life cannot destroy its meaning because nothing from the past is irretrievably lost. Everything is irrevocably stored.

COLLEAGUE: To change the subject, someone once said you were a lifelong punster.

FRANKL: Punning and other forms of humor have been among my pleasures. Many times I am offered a second cup of tea. I decline it by saying, "No, thanks. I am a mono-tea-ist. I only drink *one* cup."

COLLEAGUE: You loved climbing in the mountains.

FRANKL: Every important decision I have made, almost without exception, I have made in the mountains.

Viktor and Elly, 1958. Source: Viktor Frankl Institute, Vienna, Austria.

COLLEAGUE: You climbed until you were eighty.

FRANKL: It was my most passionate hobby.

COLLEAGUE: You knew Freud, yet you were opposed to his ideas.

FRANKL: Those who know me also know that my opposition to Freud's ideas never kept me from showing him the respect he deserves.

COLLEAGUE: You have much praise for your wife Elly.

FRANKL: The sacrifices of Elly may be even greater than my own. So that I might complete my life's work, she has denied herself much. She is the counterpart to me, both quantitatively and qualitatively. What I accomplish with my brain she fulfills with her heart.

Elly Frankl, 1964. Source: Frankl, V.E. (1997). Viktor Frankl Recollections. An Autobiography.

Jacob Needleman once said, referring to the way in which Elly has been my companion on lecture tours, "She is the warmth that accompanies the light."

COLLEAGUE: How did you meet her?

At the wedding with Leonore Schwindt, 1947. Source: Viktor Frankl Institute, Vienna, Austria.

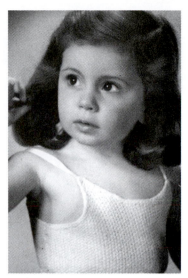

Franz and Gabriele, 1966.

Gabriele, Frankl's daughter, 1950.

FRANKL: It was 1946, and surrounded by my medical staff I made rounds in the neurology sections of the Polyclinic. I had just left one sickroom and was about to enter the next, when a young nurse approached me. She asked, on behalf of her supervisor in Oral Surgery, if I could spare a bed from my department for a patient who had just had surgery. I agreed,

Frankl and family, 1996.
Source: Klingberg, H. (2001). When Life Calls Out to Us.
The Love and Lifework of Viktor and Elly Frankl.

Frankl meets Pope Paul VI, 1970.
Source: Viktor Frankl Institute, Vienna, Austria.

and she left with a grateful smile. I turned to my assistant: "Did you see those eyes?"

COLLEAGUE: And?

FRANKL: In 1947 that nurse became my wife, Eleonore Katharina, née Schwindt.

COLLEAGUE: And the rest of your family?

FRANKL: We have a daughter, Gabriele. Our son-in-law is Franz Vesely, professor of physics at the University of Vienna. We have two grandchildren, Katharina and Alexander.

COLLEAGUE: Tell me the story of your meeting with the Pope.

The Frankls with their grandchildren.

The Frankls on the Rax Mountain.
Source: Frankl, V.E. (1997). Viktor Frankl Recollections.
An Autobiography.

FRANKL: My wife Elly was with me for the audience with the Pope, and we were both deeply impressed. Pope Paul VI greeted us in German and continued in Italian, with a priest as interpreter. He acknowledged the significance of Logotherapy for the Catholic Church and for all humankind. He also commended my conduct in the concentration camps, but it was unclear to us what he had in mind. As he signaled the end of the audience, and as we were moving toward the door, he suddenly began to speak in German once again, calling after us—to me, the Jewish neurologist from Vienna—in exactly these words: "Please pray for me!" It was deeply stirring.

The Frankls with Jerry Long, 1991.

COLLEAGUE: And if you had it to do all over again?

FRANKL: Live as if you were already living for the second time, and as if you had made the mistakes you are about to make now. That's all.

End of Scene 21

Scene 22

General Philosophy

Title Board:	**GENERAL PHILOSOPHY**
	Summarizing his life
	Meaning
	Colleague; Frankl
Visual:	Series of thoughtful Frankl photos.
Stage Directions:	Chorale from Beethoven's Ninth Symphony softly in the background. Portions in italics are not meant to be performed.

COLLEAGUE: Your writings and your lectures have been as much philosophical as they have been psychological.

FRANKL: Is there a difference?

COLLEAGUE: Perhaps not. Yet the central theme of your life has been a search for meaning.

FRANKL: In finding meaning we are perceiving a possibility in reality. Once we have actualized the possibility offered by a situation, once we have fulfilled the meaning a situation holds, we have converted that possibility into reality. And we have done so once and forever!

COLLEAGUE: *This search for meaning is almost inherent.*

FRANKL: *Yes, I understand the primordial anthropological fact that being human is always being directed, and pointing, to something or someone other than oneself: to a meaning to fulfill or another human being to encounter, a cause to serve or a person to love. Only to the extent that someone is living out this self-transcendence of human existence, is he truly human or does he become his true self. He becomes so, not only by concerning himself with his self's actualization, but by forgetting himself and giving himself, overlooking himself and focusing outward.*

COLLEAGUE: You've talked about this focusing outward—are meanings unique?

FRANKL: They are unique, they are ever-changing, but they are never missing. Life is never lacking a meaning.

COLLEAGUE: Even when you can't change a situation?

FRANKL: Yes, even then. When we are no longer able to change a situation, we are challenged to change ourselves.

COLLEAGUE: Always the inner search, always asking questions.

FRANKL: Life is asking us questions day by day, and we have to answer. Life, I would say, is a life-long question-and-answer period. As to the answers, I do not weary of saying we can only answer to life by answering *for* our lives. *Responding* to life means *being responsible* for our lives.

COLLEAGUE: *How do you fit this into the present, the future, and the past?*

FRANKL: *The present is the borderline between the unreality of the future and the eternal reality of the past. The present is also the borderline of eternity which is finite because it only extends to the present, to the present moment at which we choose what we want to admit into eternity.*

COLLEAGUE: *Explain more, please.*

FRANKL: *The borderline of eternity is the place where at every moment of our lives the decision is made as to what should be externalized and what should not.*

Viktor Frankl, 1954. Source: Viktor Frankl Institute, Vienna, Austria.

COLLEAGUE: *What is needed in the world?*

FRANKL: *Thousands of years ago mankind developed monotheism. Today another step is due. I would call it monanthropism. Not in the belief in the one God, but rather the awareness of the one mankind, the awareness of the unity of humanity; a unity in whose light the different colors of our skins would fade away.*

COLLEAGUE: Can you summarize the tenets of Logotherapy?

FRANKL: Logotherapy regards man as being in search of meaning and responsible for its fulfillment. Logotherapy sees its own assignment in making man conscious of "being responsible," of his "responsibleness."

COLLEAGUE: And summarizing your life?

FRANKL: You may guess at my words—"I have seen the meaning in my life in helping others to see in their lives a meaning."

COLLEAGUE: And suffering …

FRANKL: The right kind of suffering—facing your fate without flinching—is the highest achievement that has been granted to man.

COLLEAGUE: There are peak moments and moments of greatness.

FRANKL: They are connected. The greatness of a life can be measured by the greatness of a moment: the height of a mountain range is not given by the height of some valley, but by that of its tallest peak. In life, too, the peaks decide the meaningfulness of the life, and a single moment can retroactively flood an entire life with meaning.

COLLEAGUE: Some people miss out in life.

FRANKL: A person sitting in a streetcar who has the opportunity to watch a wonderful sunset, or to breathe in the rich scent of flowering acacias, and who instead goes on reading his newspaper, could at such a moment be accused of being negligent toward his obligations.

COLLEAGUE: You watched sunsets in the camps.

FRANKL: Sunsets are free, and they are freedom.

COLLEAGUE: Men talk about earning or deserving love.

FRANKL: Love is not deserved, is unmerited—it is simply grace. But love is not only grace: it is also enchantment.

COLLEAGUE: And how is life meaningful?

FRANKL: In three ways: first, through *what we give* to life in terms of our creative works; second, by *what we take* from the world in terms of our experiencing values; and third, through *the stand we take* toward a fate we no longer can change, like an incurable disease.

End of Scene 22

Scene 23

Frau Kotek

Title Board:	**FRAU KOTEK**
	A cancer patient
	Frankl; Frau Kotek
Visual:	Lecture hall, old woman, outside of hospital, Frankl.
Stage Directions:	This is a dialogue with an eighty-year-old female patient who is suffering from a cancer which had metastasized. Several shots of woman and Frankl, cutting back and forth.

FRANKL: What do you think of when you look back on your life? Has life been worth living?

FRAU KOTEK: Well, Doctor, I must say that I had a good life. Life was nice, indeed. And I must thank the Lord for what it held for me. I went to theaters, I attended concerts, and so forth. You see, Doctor, I went there with the family in whose house I had served for many decades as a maid, in Prague, at first, and afterwards in Vienna. And for the grace of all of these wonderful experiences I am grateful to the Lord.

FRANKL: You are speaking of some wonderful experiences; but all of this will have to end now, won't it?

FRAU KOTEK: [*Thoughtfully.*] In fact, now everything ends …

FRANKL: Well, do you think now that all of the wonderful things of your life might be annihilated and invalidated when your end approaches? [*And she knew that it did!*]

FRAU KOTEK: [*Still more thoughtfully.*] All those wonderful things …

Frankl, 1994.

FRANKL: But tell me: do you think anyone can undo the happiness, for example, that you have experienced? Can anyone blot it out?

FRAU KOTEK: [*Now facing him.*] You are right, Doctor; nobody can blot it out!

FRANKL: Or can anyone blot out the goodness you have met in your life?

FRAU KOTEK: [*Becoming increasingly emotionally involved.*] Nobody can blot it out!

FRANKL: What you have achieved and accomplished—

FRAU KOTEK: Nobody can blot it out!

FRANKL: Or what you have bravely and honestly suffered: can anyone remove it from the world—remove from the past wherein you have stored it, as it were?

FRAU KOTEK: [*Now moved to tears.*] No one can remove it. [*Pause.*] It is true, I had so much to suffer; but I also tried to be courageous and steadfast in taking life's blows. You see, Doctor, I regarded my suffering as a punishment. I believe in God.

FRANKL: But cannot suffering sometimes also be a challenge? Is it not conceivable that God wanted to see how Anastasia Kotek will bear it? And perhaps He had to admit: "Yes, she did so very bravely." And now tell me: can anyone remove such an achievement and accomplishment from the world, Frau Kotek?

FRAU KOTEK: Certainly no one can do it!

FRANKL: This remains, doesn't it?

FRAU KOTEK: It does!

FRANKL: By the way, you had no children, had you?

Frankl rock-climbing. Source: Viktor Frankl Institute, Vienna, Austria.

FRAU KOTEK: I had none.

FRANKL: Well, do you think that life is meaningful only when one has children?

FRAU KOTEK: If they are good children, why shouldn't it be a blessing?

FRANKL: Right, but you should not forget that, for instance, the greatest philosopher of all times, Immanuel Kant, had no children; but would anyone venture to doubt the extraordinary meaningfulness of his life? I rather think if children were the only meaning of life, life would become meaningless, because to procreate something which in itself is meaningless certainly would be the most meaningless thing. What counts and matters in life is rather to achieve and accomplish something. And this is precisely what you have done. You have made the best of your suffering. You have become an example for our patients by the way and manner in which you take your suffering upon yourself. I congratulate you on behalf of this achievement and accomplishment, and I also congratulate your roommates who have an opportunity to watch and witness such an example. [*Addressing students.*] *Ecce homo!* [*The*

101

audience now bursts into a spontaneous applause.] This applause concerns you, Frau Kotek. [*She is weeping now.*] It concerns your life, which has been a great achievement and accomplishment. You may be proud of it, Frau Kotek. And how few people may be proud of their lives. [*Pause.*] I should say your life is a monument. And no one can remove it from the world.

FRAU KOTEK: [*Regaining her self-control.*] What you have said, Professor Frankl, is a consolation. It comforts me. Indeed, I never had an opportunity to hear anything like this. [*Pause.*]

[*Slowly and quietly she leaves the lecture hall.*]

FRANKL: Apparently, she now was reassured. A week later she died; like Job, one could say, "in a full age." During the last week of her life, however, she was no longer depressed, but, on the contrary, full of faith and pride! Prior to this, she had admitted to Dr Gerda Becker, who was in charge of her on the ward, that she felt agonized and, more specifically, ridden by the anxiety that she was useless. The interview, however, which we had together had made her aware that her life was meaningful and that even her suffering had not been in vain. Her last words, immediately before her death, were the following: "My life is a monument. So Professor Frankl said to the whole audience, to all the students in the lecture hall. My life was not in vain." Thus reads the report of Dr Becker. And we may be justified in assuming that, also like Job, Frau Kotek "came to her grave like a shock of corn cometh in his season."

Frankl lecturing, 1960. Source: Viktor Frankl Institute, Vienna, Austria.

End of Scene 23

Scene 24

The Science Teacher

Title Board:	**THE SCIENCE TEACHER**
	Science Teacher; Frankl
Visual:	Thirteen-year-old Frankl.
Stage Directions:	Last scene in play. Blackout followed by Frankl climbing photograph and lecturing. End with good photo of Frankl and a tape recording of some lines from one of his speeches over the visual.

SCIENCE TEACHER: I must emphasize the findings of science. You see, life in the final analysis is nothing but a combustion process, an oxidation process.

FRANKL: [*Jumping to his feet.*] Professor Fritz, if this be the case, what meaning does life have?

End of Scene 24

Finis

Ericksonian Approaches
A Comprehensive Manual
Rubin Battino, M.S. & Thomas L. South, Ph.D.

A highly acclaimed, outstanding training manual in the art of Ericksonian hypnotherapy. Designed to be easily accessible, it provides a systematic approach to learning set against a clinical background, developing the reader's learning over twenty-two chapters that include the history of hypnosis, myths and misconceptions, rapport-building skills, language forms, basic and advanced inductions, utilization of ideodynamic responses, basic and advanced metaphor, and Ericksonian approaches in medicine, dentistry, substance abuse and life-challenging diseases.

Also available: a companion audiotape – ISBN 189983642X 62 mins.

"This book should undoubtedly be read and re-read by any who consider themselves to be hypnotherapists. But it should not be limited to them. If people who are not interested in the subject of hypnotherapy are not drawn to it, this will be a loss for anyone who uses language in the course of therapeutic work ... I highly recommend this book."
—*Barry Winbolt, The New Therapist.*

Thomas L. South, Ph.D. has his doctorate in clinical psychology from the Union Institute. He has conducted workshops for the Associate Trainers in Clinical Hypnosis, and has developed and taught courses in Ericksonian approaches at the University of Dayton and with Rubin Battino at Wright State University. He invited the faculty at the Third International Congress on Ericksonian Approaches to Hypnosis and Psychotherapy. He is the author of a chapter entitled "Hypnosis in Childbirth: A Case Study in Anesthesia." Dr. South is the founder and first president of the Milton H. Erickson Society of Dayton, and is presently a staff psychologist at the Twin Valley Psychiatric System—Dayton Forensic Unit. He has had a private practice for many years.

CLOTH   564 PAGES   ISBN: 1899836314

Guided Imagery
And Other Approaches To Healing
Rubin Battino, M.S.

An essentially practical and accessible healing manual, *Guided Imagery* presents a breakdown of published guided imagery scripts, while investigating the language used in guided imagery, the skills required in rapport-building, and the most effective methods in inducing a state of relaxation. Pioneering new bonding and fusion healing methods, *Guided Imagery* also incorporates a useful section on preparing patients for surgery, and a chapter on Nutrition and Healing, by nutrition expert A. Ira Fritz, Ph.D., plus a chapter on Native American Healing Traditions, by Native American healer Helena Sheehan, Ph.D. Designed as a resource for health professionals, *Guided Imagery*, meticulously researched and authoritative, is essential reading for doctors, nurses, psychologists, counselors and all those involved or interested in healing.

"Well chosen, illuminating clinical examples abound, with eminently useful imagery suggestions for practitioner and patient."
—*Belleruth Naparstek, L.I.S.W., author of Staying Well with Guided Imagery.*

Also available: 2 audiotape set of guided imagery scripts, 113 mins. ISBN: 1899836594

Rubin Battino, M.S. has a private practice in Yellow Springs, Ohio. He teaches courses periodically for the Department of Human Services at Wright State University where he holds the rank of adjunct professor. He has over six years of experience as a facilitator in a Bernie Siegel style support group for people who have life-threatening diseases and those who support them. He is President of the Milton H. Erickson Society of Dayton, co-chair of an ad hoc committee to establish certification standards for training in Ericksonian hypnotherapy for the societies and institutes affiliated with the Milton H. Erickson Foundation. He has developed and teaches courses in Ericksonian hypnotherapy at Wright State University with T.L. South. He is Professor Emeritus of chemistry.

CLOTH   400 PAGES   ISBN: 1899836446

Coping
A Practical Guide for People with
Life-Challenging Diseases and their Caregivers
Rubin Battino, M.S.

Coping is a practical guide for those living with or dealing with life-challenging diseases. Detailing the many effective coping strategies that Professor Rubin Battino has encountered during his extensive professional experience—from friends and support groups, from research and from practice—it is written to be thoroughly accessible and informative, inviting you to explore a wide range of techniques and methods that have proved to have a healing influence.

"Coping is an excellent source of information and wisdom, and when they are combined with action and inspiration wonderful things happen."
 —*Bernie Siegel, M.D. author of Love, Medicine & Miracles and Prescriptions for Living.*

PAPERBACK   192 PAGES   ISBN: 1899836683

Metaphoria
Metaphor and Guided Metaphor for
Psychotherapy and Healing
Rubin Battino, M.S.

In this groundbreaking book, Rubin Battino provides the reader with the definitive guide to metaphor and its use as a therapeutic tool. This is an essential text for training and professional use, and for *anyone* serious about exploring the potential of metaphor. Conducting a systematic analysis of the effectiveness of metaphor, *Metaphoria* examines:

- the structure of a metaphor: from its essential elements to its optional components
- the delivery of metaphor: from rapport-building and communication skills to the art of effective story-telling
- what makes a metaphor work, with examples of poor and good usage.

Forming a complete reference and resource for the practitioner and therapist, *Metaphoria* investigates:

- the application of metaphors: for children, geriatrics, sleep induction, pain control, trauma, and other purposes
- language forms—the words, phrases and grammatical structure that enhance the content of a metaphor
- the relation of Ericksonian psychotherapy and hypnosis to metaphor
- themes and ideas for metaphor
- the use of metaphors in specific approaches such as: reframing, art therapies, hypnotherapy, healing, preparation for surgery, narrative therapy, solution-focused therapy, and ordeal therapy.

Containing sample scripts and suggestions for basic and advanced metaphors, plus a history of the use of metaphor, *Metaphoria* provides the reader with everything they need to comprehend fully the metaphor's unique properties, and create metaphors for their own unique purposes. The new authority on the subject, *Metaphoria* provides a complete anatomy of the metaphor, and a creative and comprehensive guide to its applications.

"A must-buy and must-read book. Rubin's freshness and honesty is unparalleled, his grasp of the subject matter is uncanny."
—*Stephen Lankton*

CLOTH   376 PAGES   ISBN: 1899836829

USA & Canada *orders to:*

Crown House Publishing
P.O. Box 2223, Williston, VT 05495-2223, USA
Tel: 877-925-1213, Fax: 802-864-7626
www.crownhouse.co.uk

UK & Rest of World *orders to:*

The Anglo American Book Company Ltd.
Crown Buildings, Bancyfelin, Carmarthen, Wales SA33 5ND
Tel: +44 (0)1267 211880/211886, Fax: +44 (0)1267 211882
E-mail: books@anglo-american.co.uk
www.anglo-american.co.uk

Australasia *orders to:*

Footprint Books Pty Ltd
101 McCarrs Creek Road, P.O. Box 418, Church Point
Sydney NSW 2105, Australia
Tel: +61 2 9997 3973, Fax: +61 2 9997 3185
E-mail: footprintbooks@ozmail.com.au